S.F.B.Morse Pinxt. S.S.Jocelyn Se

JEREMY L. CROSS.

THE TRUE

Masonic Chart,

OR

HIEROGLYPHIC MONITOR;

CONTAINING

ALL THE EMBLEMS EXPLAINED

IN THE DEGREES OF

ENTERED APPRENTICE, FELLOW CRAFT, MASTER. MASON, MARK MASTER, PAST MASTER, MOST EXCELLENT MASTER, ROYAL ARCH, ROYAL MASTER, AND SELECT MASTER:

DESIGNED AND DULY ARRANGED AGREEABLY TO THE

LECTURES,

BY R. W. JEREMY L. CROSS, G. L.

TO WHICH ARE ADDED,

Illustrations, Charges, Songs, &c.

With Additions and Emendations; and the Emblems newly designed and improved.

STONE GUILD PUBLISHING
PLANO, TEXAS
HTTP://WWW.STONEGUILDPUBLISHING.COM/

2009

Originally Published By:
T.G. WOODWARD AND COMPANY
1826

Plano, Texas
http://www.stoneguildpublishing.com/

First Paperback Edition 2009

ISBN-13 978-1-60532-043-4
ISBN-10 1-60532-043-9

10 9 8 7 6 5 4 3 2

DISTRICT OF CONNECTICUT, to wit:

BE it remembered, That on the fifth day of August, in the fifty-first year of the Independence of the United States of America, A. D. 1826, JEREMY L. CROSS, of the said District, hath deposited in this Office the Title of a Book, the right whereof he claims as author; in the words following—to wit:

"The True Masonic Chart, or Hieroglyphic Monitor, containing all the Emblems explained in the degrees of Entered Apprentice, Fellow Craft. Master Mason, Mark Master, Past Master, Most Excellent Master, Royal Arch, Royal Master, and Select Master; designed and duly arranged agreeably to the Lectures, by R. W. JEREMY L. CROSS, G. L. To which are added. Illustrations. Charges, Songs, &c. Fourth Edition. with additions and emendations; with; the Emblems newly designed and improved"—

In conformity to the act of the Congress of the United States, entitled "An act for the encouragement of learning, by securing the copies of maps, charts and books, to the authors and proprietors of such copies, during the times therein mentioned"—and also to the act entitled "An act supplementary to an act entitled 'An act for the encouragement of learning, by securing the copies of maps, charts, and books, to the authors and proprietors of such copies, during the times therein mentioned,' and extending the benefits thereof to the arts of designing, engraving, and etching historical and other prints."

CHAS. A. INGERSOLL,
Clerk of the District of Connecticut.

PROSTYLE TEMPLE.
HIRAM.
SOLOMON.
JOSHUA
SHEM.
HAM.
MOSES.
AHOLIAB.

TO THE

OFFICERS

OF THE

General Grand Chapter

OF THE

UNITED STATES OF AMERICA,

THIS LITTLE VOLUME

IS

RESPECTFULLY DEDICATED,

BY

The Author.

PREFACE.

HAVING been honored by the approbation of the Officers of the General Grand Chapter of the United States, and of most of the Grand Lodges, and Officers of Grand Lodges, in the individual States, as a Grand Lecturer;—and having, by virtue of their sanction and authority, officiated in that capacity for several years; the Author of this volume has had an opportunity of witnessing the mode of lecturing, and working, in many different Lodges. It is not surprising, therefore, if, in the course of his experience, some errors in the practice of these branches should have fallen within his observation. These have undoubtedly originated from a want of uniformity; and although they may not be considered as radical evils, in relation to the hidden mysteries of the Fraternity, yet they would certainly be regarded as defects in that system, the perfect preservation of which, is at once the pride and glory of every enlightened mason.

Among these errors may be mentioned,—the improper classification of Masonic emblems; and a difference in the mode of working.

To obviate these inaccuracies, is the object of this work. It contains a classification of the emblems, together with illustrations, that have been approved and adopted by a majority of the Lodges of the United States. So far, therefore, as they are connected with the mode of working, and of lecturing, the evils which have been suggested, will be obviated by an attention to this treatise: and so far only does the Author claim any merit in having contributed towards establishing a standard, which he flatters himself may serve as a safe and sure guide to his Brethren, in some parts of their labors.

The illustrations, &c. are selected from the compilations of Preston, Webb, and other established authorities, accompanied by such alterations and emendations, as were deemed necessary to a strict conformity with the *Ancient System.*

With a hope that his exertions to benefit them may not prove fruitless, the Author respectfully submits his work TO THE FRATERNITY OF FREE AND ACCEPTED MASONS THROUGHOUT THE UNITED STATES.

PREFACE TO THE THIRD EDITION.

SINCE the publication of the first edition of the MASONIC CHART, it has been adopted as a Text—Book by most of the Lodges and Chapters in this country.

The highest expectations of the author have been more than realized in the reception of the first and second editions by his Masonic Brethren. Its beneficial effects in promoting uniformity in our mode of working and lecturing have induced him to present to the Fraternity the third edition, with some additions and emendations. If his labors shall in any degree contribute to the advancement of a Society, in which he feels a lively interest, he will be abundantly compensated. It has been his constant aim to place the Masonic Institution upon its proper basis. The correct Mason will ever be more esteemed than the over—zealous or coldly indifferent members of the Society. A Mason who is thoroughly acquainted with the tenets and nature of this Institution, ranks it among the first of human origin, and as inculcating the purest of moral principles, and as having a powerful tendency, where strict discipline is judiciously administered agreeably to the tenets of the Institution, to improve the morals of its members, and to open and expand their hearts to acts of charity and pure benevolence. Those who elevate masonry to a level with revealed religion, and those who rank it below the standard of pure morality, are equally unacquainted with its true object.

That every Brother and Companion may possess a correct knowledge of the nature and principles of our excellent Institution, and that their conduct may be such through life as to convince all with whom they may have intercourse, that our great aim is to inculcate FRIENDSHIP, MORALITY, BROTHERLY LOVE, and CHARITY, is the earnest and sincere wish of

THE AUTHOR.

ADVERTISEMENT.

IN presenting the fourth edition of the Masonic Chart to the Fraternity, the Author is happy to state that but few alterations in the last edition are necessary, except in the Emblems and Hieroglyphics, which are much improved by new designs, emendations and additions. While he believes the work has been much improved in accordance with the principles of the Institution, he yet feels conscious that some defects may be discovered by the scrutinizing eye of his more experienced Brethren; he would therefore solicit their forbearance and candor. In taking a retrospective view of the Institution, it is truly gratifying to every upright and correct Mason, to notice the great improvement which has been made within a few years past.—In an institution like ours, however, which is founded on the MORAL LAW OF GOD, and requires that all her members should walk in accordance thereto, we can easily discern that much remains to be done—Especially should it not be forgotten that the very nature of the Institution forbids the admission of any to membership, except men sustaining the straightest moral character, and that no Lodge can be justified in receiving candidates solely for the purpose of increasing their members or their funds.—Let them strictly adhere to the Masonic rule, and let the "internal and not the external qualifications of the man" be the standard for admission. As every man, on entering a Lodge, first puts his trust in GOD, and then takes the "HOLY SCRIPTURES to be the rule and guide of his faith and practice," so none should be suffered to remain members who deviate there from.

It is the intention of the Author of this little volume, by the leave of Divine Providence, to present to his Masonic Brethren, as soon as convenient, a new and improved edition of the "MASONIC BOOK OF CONSTITUTIONS," a work which is often alluded to, but seldom seen, except in a few Lodges. It is designed to give a brief History of Masonry from its commencement up to the present time, comprising also observations on the regulations of Lodges, duties of Officers, admission of Candidates, duty of Discipline, forms of Petitions, Warrants, Charters, &c. &c. with a complete list of all the Encampments,

Councils, Chapters and Lodges in the United States. The Author is well aware that in many parts of our country, which have been highly favored with Masonic light and knowledge, a work of this kind would be of minor consequence, but there are many sections which have not been thus highly favored, and where it would tend to advance the true interests of the Institution.

The Author would improve this favorable opportunity in calling upon all Christian Masons to lend their aid in elevating the Institution to its proper level, by influencing every Mason by example, exhortation and persuasion, to live up to the moral precepts which are inculcated in it.—At the same time to guard them against relying on any merit in their own works as a title to that REST beyond the grave, which is prepared for the children of God,—and to point them to HIM, who is the WAY, the TRUTH and the LIFE—to the LION of the tribe of Judah, to the great WATCHMAN of Israel, to our DIVINE REDEEMER, whose name is the only name which is given under Heaven whereby men can be saved—who has made an atonement for sin by the shedding of his own blood, and who has promised that whosoever believeth on Him shall not perish but have everlasting life.

That all his Brethren may not only be found *Worthy, Free and Accepted Masons,* but qualified by the SPIRIT of our GOD for a seat in that House not made with hands, Eternal in the Heavens, is the earnest prayer of

THE AUTHOR.

INTRODUCTION.

Form of a PETITION to be signed by a Candidate for Initiation.

TO the W. Master, Wardens, and Brethren of —— — Lodge, No. ——, of Free and Accepted Masons.

The subscriber, residing in ———, of lawful age, and by occupation a ———, begs leave to state, that, unbiased by friends, and uninfluenced by mercenary motives, he freely and voluntarily offers himself as a candidate for the mysteries of masonry, and that he is prompted to solicit this privilege by a favorable opinion conceived of the Institution, a desire of knowledge, and a sincere wish of being serviceable to his fellow creatures. Should his petition be granted, he will cheerfully conform to all the ancient established usages and customs of the Fraternity.

(Signed) A. B.

The following Recommendation is to be signed by two members of the Lodge to which the application is made:

THIS may certify, that we the subscribers are personally acquainted with Mr. A. B.; and from a confidence in his integrity, and the uprightness of his intention, do cheerfully recommend and propose him as a proper candidate for the mysteries of Masonry.

Recommended by C. D.
Avouched for by E. F.

ON OPENING AND CLOSING LODGES.

THE ceremony of opening and closing a Lodge with solemnity and decorum is universally admitted among Masons: and though the mode in some Lodges may vary, and in every degree must, in some particulars, still uniformity prevails in every Lodge; and the variations, if any, are only occasioned by want of method, which a little application might easily remove. To conduct this ceremony with propriety ought to be the study of every Mason, but more especially those who are called to officiate as officers of the Lodge. To those of our brethren who are thus honored, every eye is naturally directed for propriety of conduct and behavior; and from them, our brethren who are less informed will expect an example worthy of imitation. From a share in this ceremony, no mason can be exempted: it is a general concern, in which all must assist; the first notice of which is given by the W. M. with a request of the attention and assistance of his brethren. No sooner has it been signified, than every officer repairs to his station, and the brethren rank according to their degrees. The next object is to detect impostors among ourselves, and for this purpose recourse is had to our peculiar rites as masons. This object being accomplished, our next care is directed to the external avenues of the Lodge, and the proper officers, whose province it is to discharge that duty, execute their trust with fidelity, and by certain mystic forms, of no recent date, intimate that we may safely precede.

At opening the Lodge, two purposes are wisely affected; the master is reminded of the dignity of character which he is to maintain from the elevation of his office and the brethren of the reverence and respect due from them in their sundry stations. These are not the only advantages resulting from a due observance of this ceremony;—the mind is drawn with reverential awe to the Supreme Architect of the Universe, and the eye fixed on HIM who is the only author of life and immortality. Here we are taught to worship and adore the supreme JEHOVAH, and to supplicate his protection and assistance in all our well-meant endeavors. After the customary salutations, the master pronounces the Lodge to be opened in due and ancient form, and assumes the government, and under him his wardens: the brethren with one accord unite in duty and respect, and the business of the meeting is conducted with order and harmony.

At the closing of a Lodge, a similar ceremony takes place as at opening;—the avenues of the Lodge are guarded; a recapitulation of the duties of the officers is rehearsed; a proper tribute of gratitude is offered up to the Great Author of our existence, and his blessing invoked and extended to the whole fraternity.

If it should be deemed necessary that the Lodge be opened in the several degrees, for dispatch of business, when that in the first degree shall have been finished, the W. Master, after due enquiry of the wardens and brethren, will proclaim it to be his will and pleasure that the Entered Apprentices degree be dispensed with for the purpose of opening on the Fellow Craft's degree, and all who are not Fellow Crafts are requested to retire. When the necessary precautions are taken that none remain but those who are entitled to this privilege, the sentinel is again reminded of his duty, and the Fellow Craft's degree opened in due form. When the business in this degree shall have been finished, the Lodge is dispensed with, as in the first degree, and a Master's Lodge opened in due form. After the business in the Master's Degree is finished, the Lodge is closed and the labors of the Fellow Craft's resumed: if nothing should offer in this degree, the Lodge is closed and the labors of the Entered Apprentices' resumed. Should nothing further offer in this degree, the records of the evening having been read and approved, the Lodge is closed in due and ancient form.

These are but faint outlines of the ceremonies which prevail among masons, in every country, and distinguish all their meetings.

FORMS OF PRAYERS, CHARGES, &c.

A Prayer used on opening a Lodge.

Most holy and glorious Lord God, the great Architect of the universe, the giver of all good gifts and graces: Thou hast promised, that "where two or three are gathered together in thy name, thou wilt be in the midst of them, and bless them." In thy name we assemble, most humbly beseeching thee to bless us in all our undertakings, that we may know and serve thee aright, and that all our actions may tend to thy glory, and to our advancement in knowledge and virtue. And we beseech thee, O Lord God, to bless our present assembling, and to illuminate our minds, through the intercession of the Son of Righteousness, that we may walk in the light of thy countenance; and when the trials of our probationary state are over, be admitted into **THE TEMPLE** "not made with hands, eternal in the heavens."

So mote it be. Amen.

A Prayer at Closing.

Supreme Architect of the universe, accept our humble praises for the many mercies and blessings which thy bounty has conferred on us, and especially for this friendly and social intercourse. Pardon, we beseech thee, whatever thou hast seen amiss in us since we have been together; and continue to us thy presence, protection, and blessing. Make us sensible of the renewed obligations we are under to love thee supremely, and to be friendly to each other. May all our irregular passions be subdued, and may we daily increase in *Faith, Hope,* and *Charity;* but more especially in that *Charity,* which is the bond of peace, and the perfection of every virtue. May we so practice thy precepts, that, through the merits of the Redeemer, we may finally obtain thy promises, and find an entrance through the gates into the temple and city of our God. So mote it be. Amen.

Benediction at Closing.

May the blessing of Heaven rest upon us and all regular masons! May brotherly love prevail, and every moral and social virtue cement us!

So mote it be. Amen.

Charge at Closing.

BRETHREN,

We are now about to quit this sacred retreat of friendship and virtue, to mix again with the world. Amidst its concerns and employments, forget not the duties which you have heard so frequently inculcated, and so forcibly recommended in this Lodge. Be diligent, prudent, temperate, discreet. Remember, that around this altar, you have promised to befriend and relieve every brother, who shall need your assistance. You have promised, in the most friendly manner to remind him of his errors, and aid a reformation. These generous principles are to extend further. Every human being has a claim upon your kind offices. Do good unto all. Recommend it more especially "to the household of the faithful." Finally, brethren, be ye all of one mind; live in peace; and may the God of love and peace delight to dwell with and bless you.

RECOMMENDATIONS.

[For the information of those of the Fraternity, with whom the Author of this little volume has not had the pleasure of an acquaintance, he would submit the following, from a large number of Certificates, in testimony of his masonic qualifications.]

TO THE FRATERNITY OF FREE AND ACCEPTED MASONS THROUGHOUT THE UNITED STATES OF NORTH-AMERICA———GREETING.

KNOW YE, That we, the undersigned, having duly examined our worthy Companion, JEREMY L. CROSS, do find him well *skilled* and correct in the Lectures and mode of working in the three first Degrees of *Ancient Free Masonry,* as received, sanctioned, and directed to be taught, by the several Grand Lodges of New—Hampshire, Massachusetts, Rhode—Island, Connecticut, Vermont, New—York, and New—Jersey. Also, with the Lectures and mode of working in the several Degrees of Mark Master, Past Master, Most Excellent Master, and Royal Arch Masonry, as sanctioned and directed to be taught by the Officers of the General Grand Royal Arch Chapter of the United States of N. America. We do therefore cheerfully recommend him as fully competent to teach the same.

Duly appreciating the utility that would arise from a greater uniformity in our mode of working and Lecturing; and as the good of the INSTITUTION demands it; we do therefore earnestly recommend to the whole FRATERNITY, to receive, sanction, and adopt the same.

Witness our Hands.

M. E. and Hon. DEWITT CLINTON, Gen. Grand High Priest of the Gen. Grand Royal Arch Chapter of the U. States of America; also Grand Master of the Grand Lodge of N. York.

M. E. HENRY FOWLE, Esq. D. G. G. H. Priest of the G. G. R. A. C. of the U. S. A.; also Deputy Grand High Priest of the Grand Chapter of Massachusetts.

M. E. THOMAS SMITH WEBB, Esq. P. D. G. G. H. Priest of the G. G. R. A. C. of the U. S. A.; also Past Grand Master of the Grand Lodge of Rhode—Island.

M. E. JOHN SNOW, Esq. G. G. King of the G. G. R. A. C. of the U. S. A.; also G. H. Priest of the Grand Chapter of Ohio.

M. E. JOHN HART LYNDE, Esq. P. G. G. King of the G. G. R. A. C. of the U. S. A.; also Past Senior G. Warden of the Grand Lodge of Connecticut.

M. E. PHILIP P. ECKEL, Esq. G. G. Scribe of the G. G. R. A. C. of the U. S. A.; also Past G. High Priest of the Grand Chapter of Maryland and District of Columbia.

M. E. PETER GRINNELL, Esq. G. G. Treasurer of the G. G. R. A. C. of the U. S. A.

M. E. OTIS AMIDON, P. G. G. Secretary of the G. G. R. A. C. of the U. S. A.

M. W. JOHN HARRIS, Grand Master,
R. W. ALBE CADY, Senior G. Warden,
R. W. STEPHEN BLANCHARD, Junior G. Warden,
R. W. HORACE CHASE, G. Lecturer,
} of the Grand Lodge of New—Hampshire.

M. W. FRANCIS J. OLIVER, G. Master,
R. W. JOHN DIXWELL, Deputy G. M. R.
W. AUGUSTUS PEABODY, Senior G. Warden,
} of the Grand Lodge of Massachusetts.

M. W. JOHN CARLILE, Grand Master of the Grand Lodge of Rhode—Island.

R. W. LYMAN LAW, Deputy G. Master,
R. W. THOMAS H. CUSHING, Senior G. Warden,
} of the Grand Lodge of Connecticut.

M. W. LEMUEL WHITNEY, G. Master of the Grand Lodge of Vermont,

M. W JAMES GILES, G. Master of the Grand Lodge of New-Jersey.

WE, the undersigned, Officers in the General Grand Royal Arch Chapter of the United States of America, DO APPROVE and RECOMMEND "The True Masonic Chart, or Hieroglyphic Monitor," designed and arranged by our worthy Companion, JEREMY L. CROSS, as entitled to the attention and use of the Craft; being a valuable assistant in elucidating the various Masonic Emblems, and enabling the diligent Craftsman to acquire the Lectures in the several degrees of *Ancient Free Masonry*.

M. E. DEWITT CLINTON, General Grand High Priest.
HENRY FOWLE, Deputy Gen. Grand High Priest.
JOHN SNOW, General Grand King.
PHILIP P. ECKEL, General Grand Scribe.
PETER GRINNELL, General Grand Treasurer.
JOHN ABBOT, General Grand Secretary.
DAVID G. COWAN, General Grand Marshal.
JOHN HARRIS, Past Gen. Grand Marshal; also M. W. G. Master of the Grand Lodge of New—Hampshire.

WE, the Subscribers. Officers of the Grand Royal Arch Chapter of Connecticut, having examined "The Masonic Chart, or Hieroglyphic Monitor," designed by our worthy Companion, R. W. JEREMY L. CROSS, for the use and instruction of the Craft, with pleasure recommend the same as a necessary and useful Manual for all Free Masons; containing an elegant and comprehensive view of all the Symbols used in Lecturing upon the several Degrees of *Ancient Masonry*.

M. E. LYMAN LAW, G. H. Priest.
M. E. LABAN SMITH, D. G. H. Priest.
E. DAVID DEMING, G. King.
E. THOMAS H. CUSHING, G. Scribe.
Comp. HENRY CHAMPION, G. Treasurer.
HORATIO G. HALE, G. Secretary.
MENZIES RAYNER, G. Chaplain.
SAMUEL GREEN, G. Marshal.

Extract from the proceedings of the Most Worshipful Grand Lodge of Connecticut, May, A. L. 5820.

RESOLVED, That this Grand Lodge approve of the Masonic Chart, published by Brother JEREMY L. CROSS, and recommend it to be used as a Masonic Text—Book in all the Lodges working under this jurisdiction.

A true copy from the minutes.

Attest—WM. H. JONES, G. Secretary.

Extract from the proceedings of the Grand Royal Arch Chapter of Connecticut, May, A. D. 1820, *and of R. A. M.* 2850.

RESOLVED, That this Grand Chapter approve of the Masonic Chart, published by Companion JEREMY L. CROSS, and recommend it to be used as a Text—Book in the several Chapters under their jurisdiction.

A true copy from the minutes.

Attest—E. GOODRICH, jun. Grand Secretary.

MASTERS CARPET

The True

MASONIC CHART,

OR

Hieroglyphic Monitor;

BY

R. W. JEREMY L. CROSS G. L.

New Haven

1826

ENTERED APPRENTICE DEGREE.

Section First.

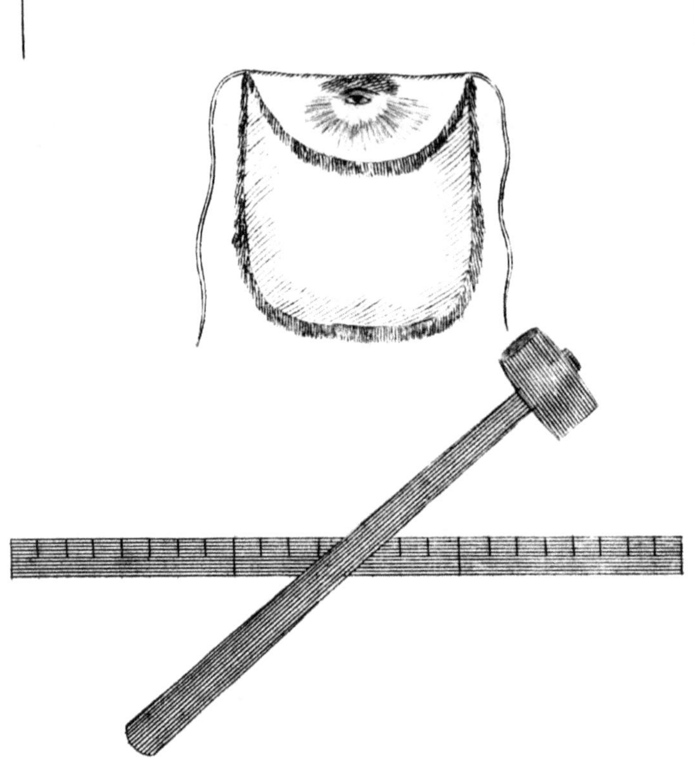

Section Second.

Section Third.

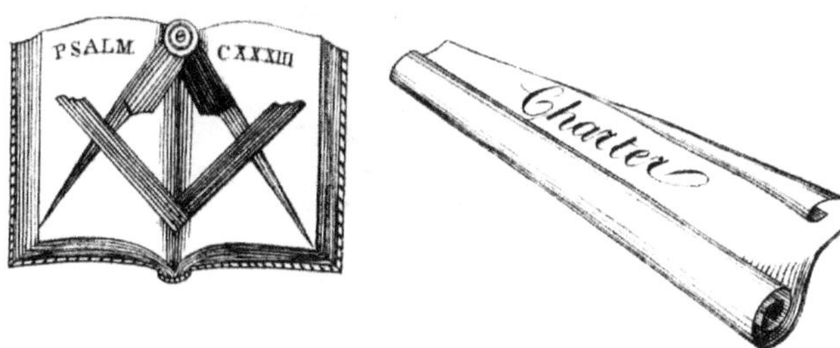

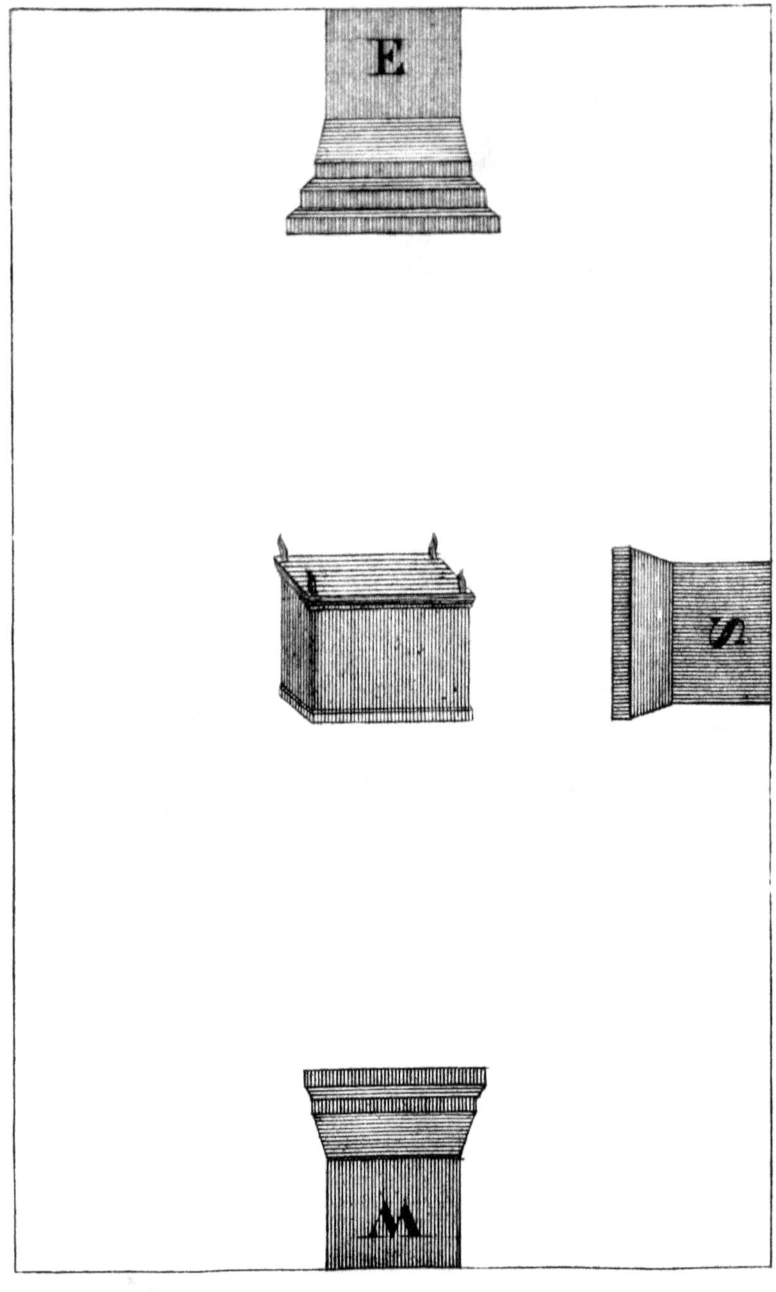
E
S
M

W
S
B

C
H
F

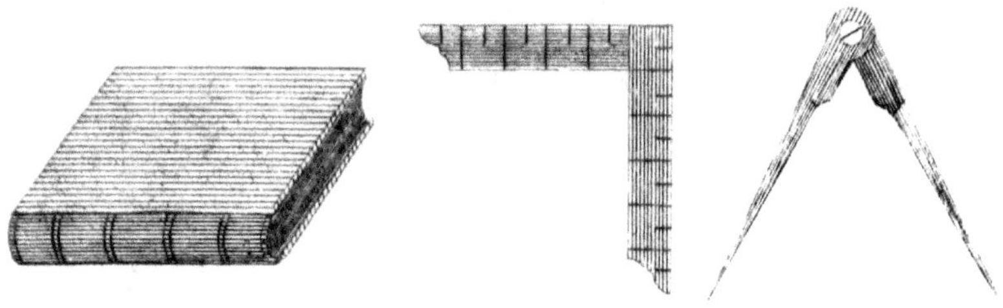

E
W
HOLY
BIBLE
B
E
T
F
P
J

FELLOW CRAFTS DEGREE.

Section First.

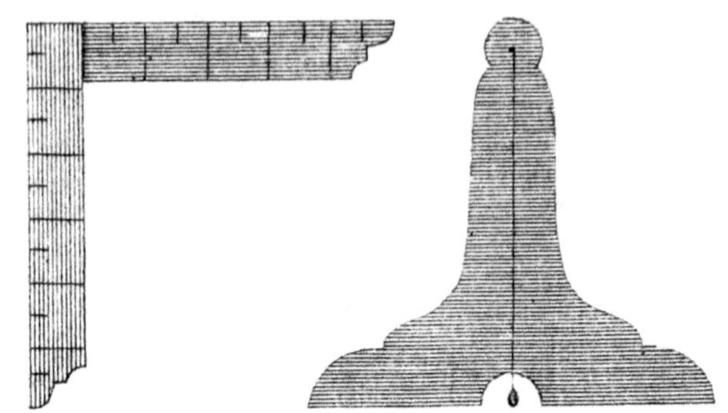

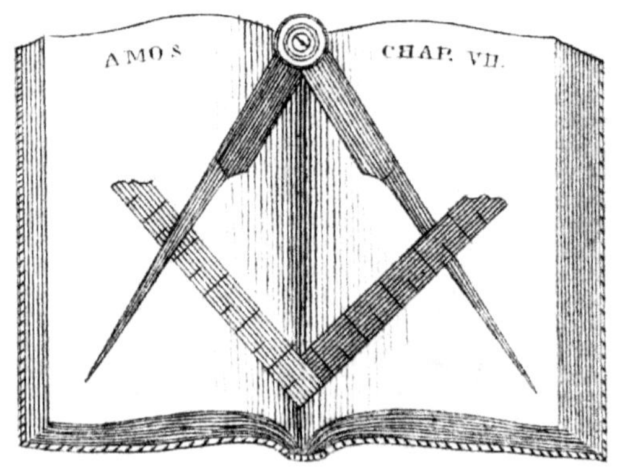

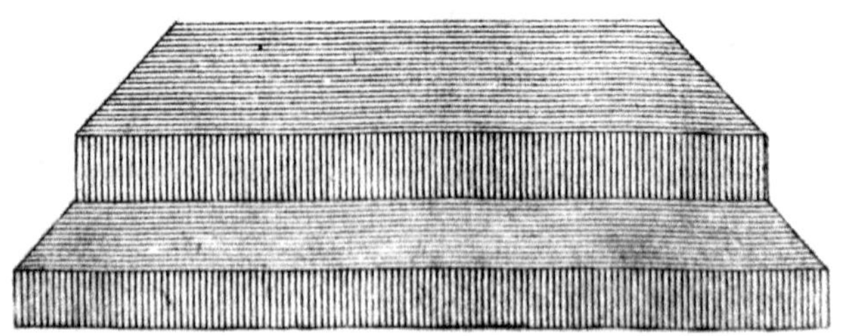

Section Second.

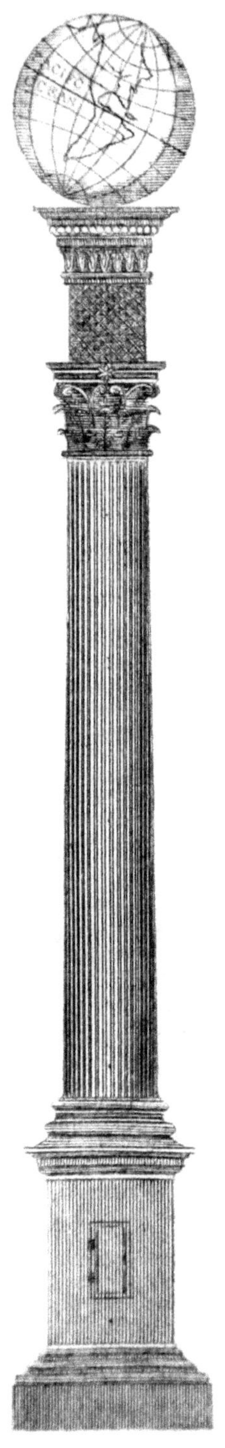

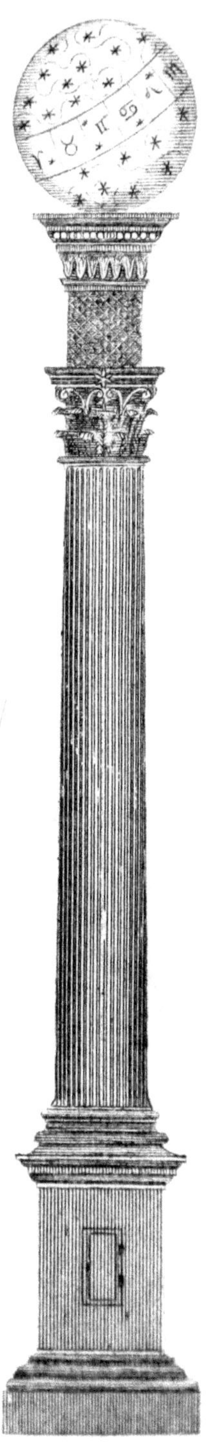

Tuscan.
Doric.
Ionic.
Corinthian.
Composite.

G

MASTER MASONS DEGREE

Section First.

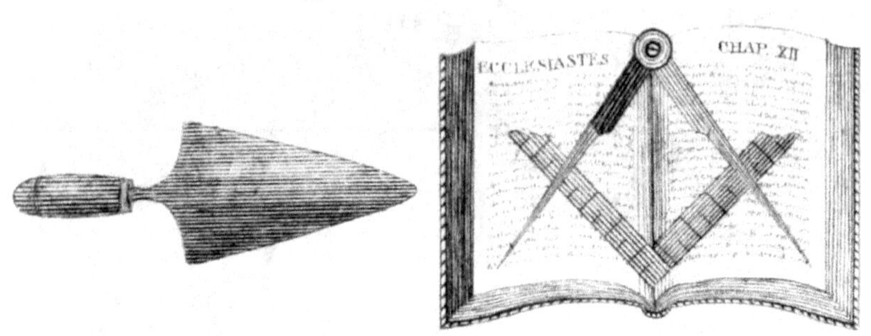

Section Second.

Section Third.

1,453. Columns.

2,906, Pilasters.

3. Grand Masters.

3,300. Overseers.

80,000. Fellow Crafts.

70,000. Entered Apprentices.

7 { 1 — 6

5 { 2 — 3

3

CONSTITUTIONS

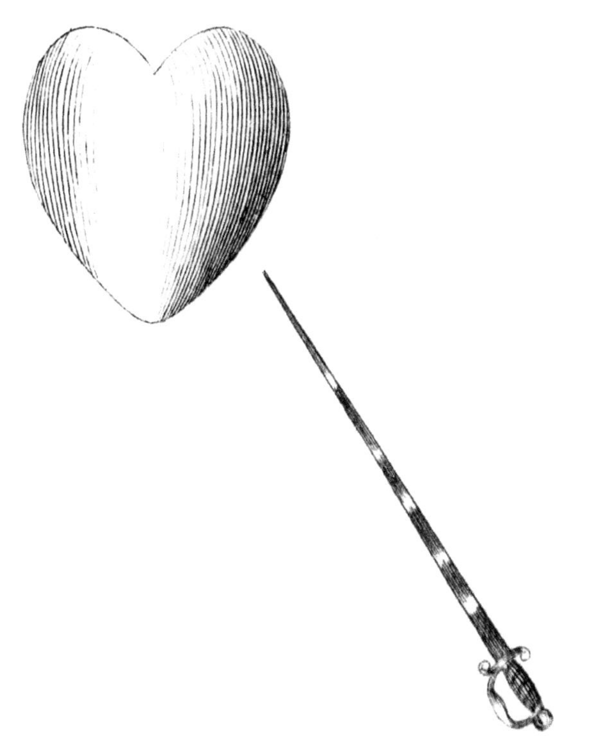

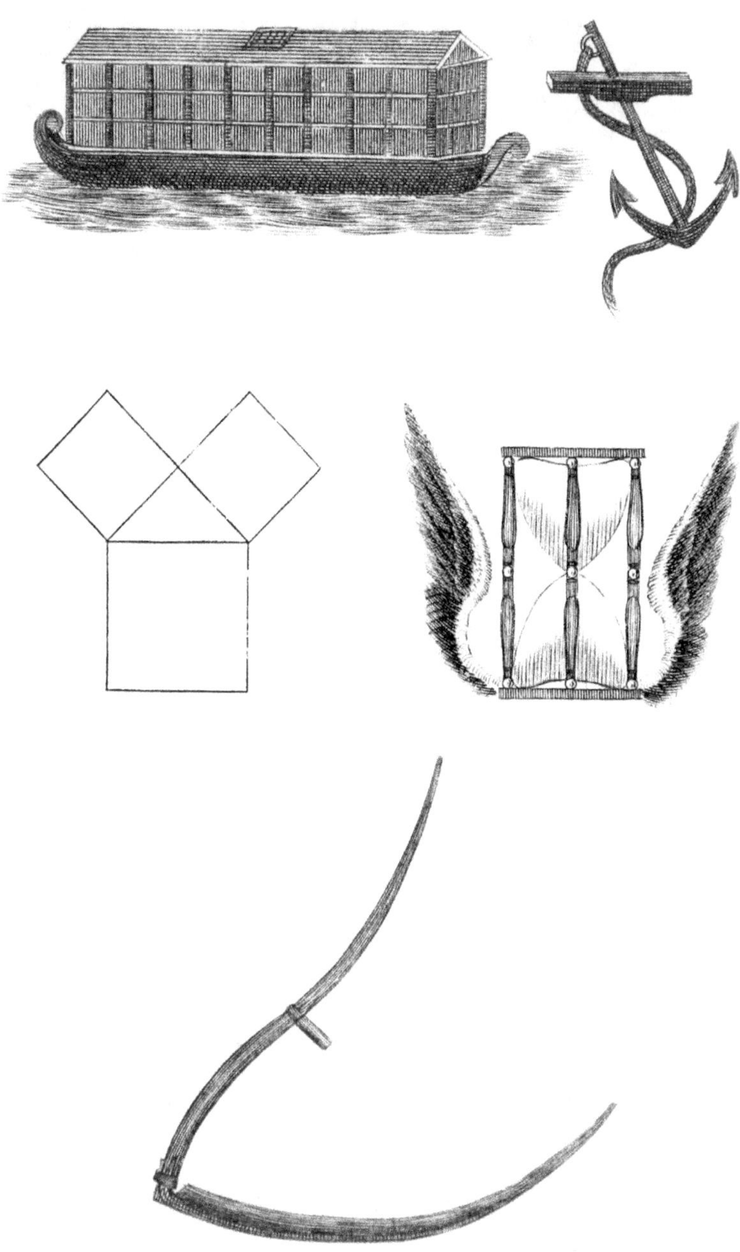

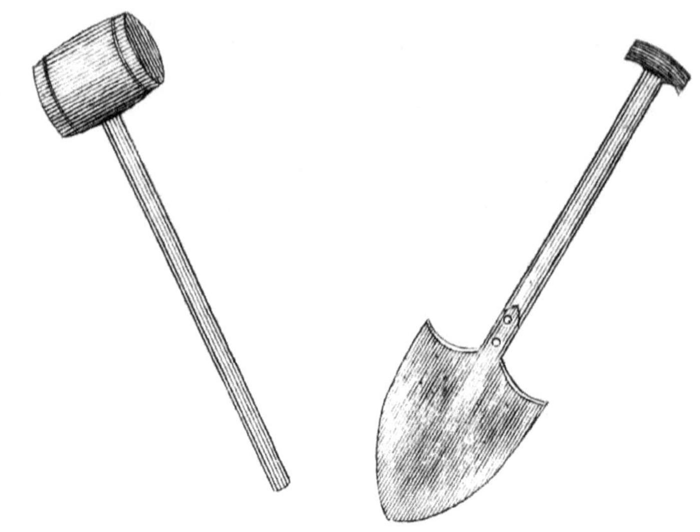

MARK MASTERS DEGREE.

Section First.

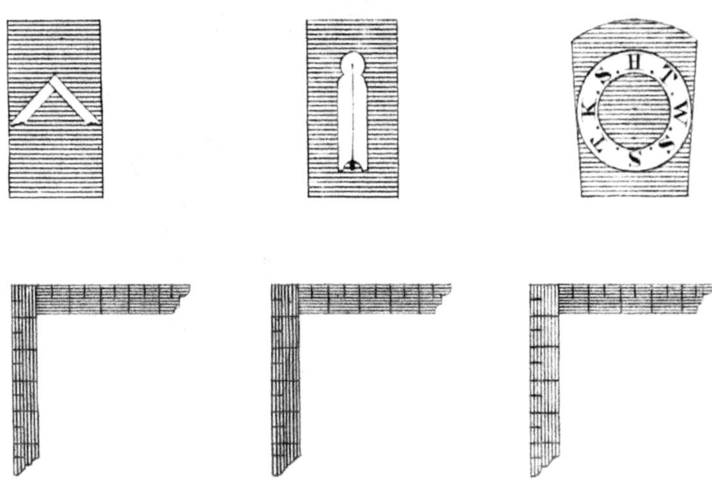

Section Second.

II Chronicles II.-XVI.

PAST MASTERS DEGREE.

MOST EXCELLENT MASTERS DEGREE.

ROYAL ARCH DEGREE.

Section First.

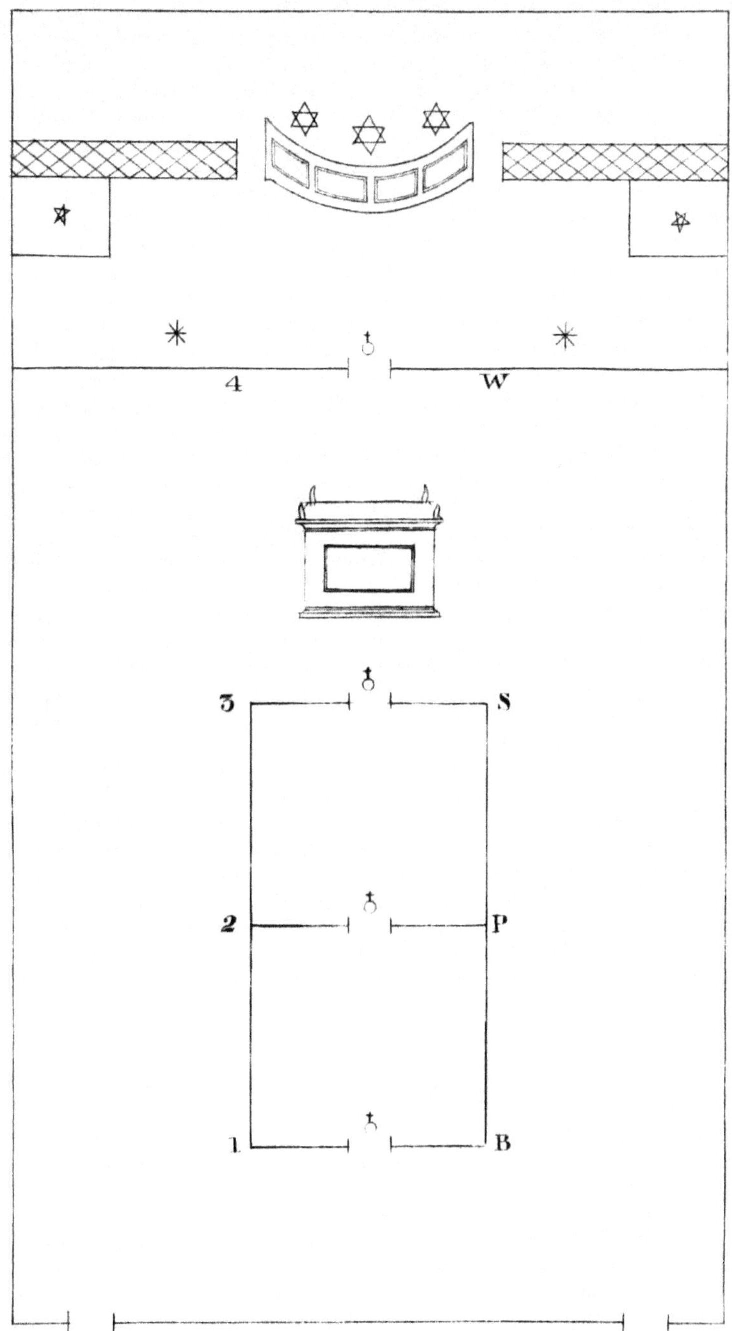

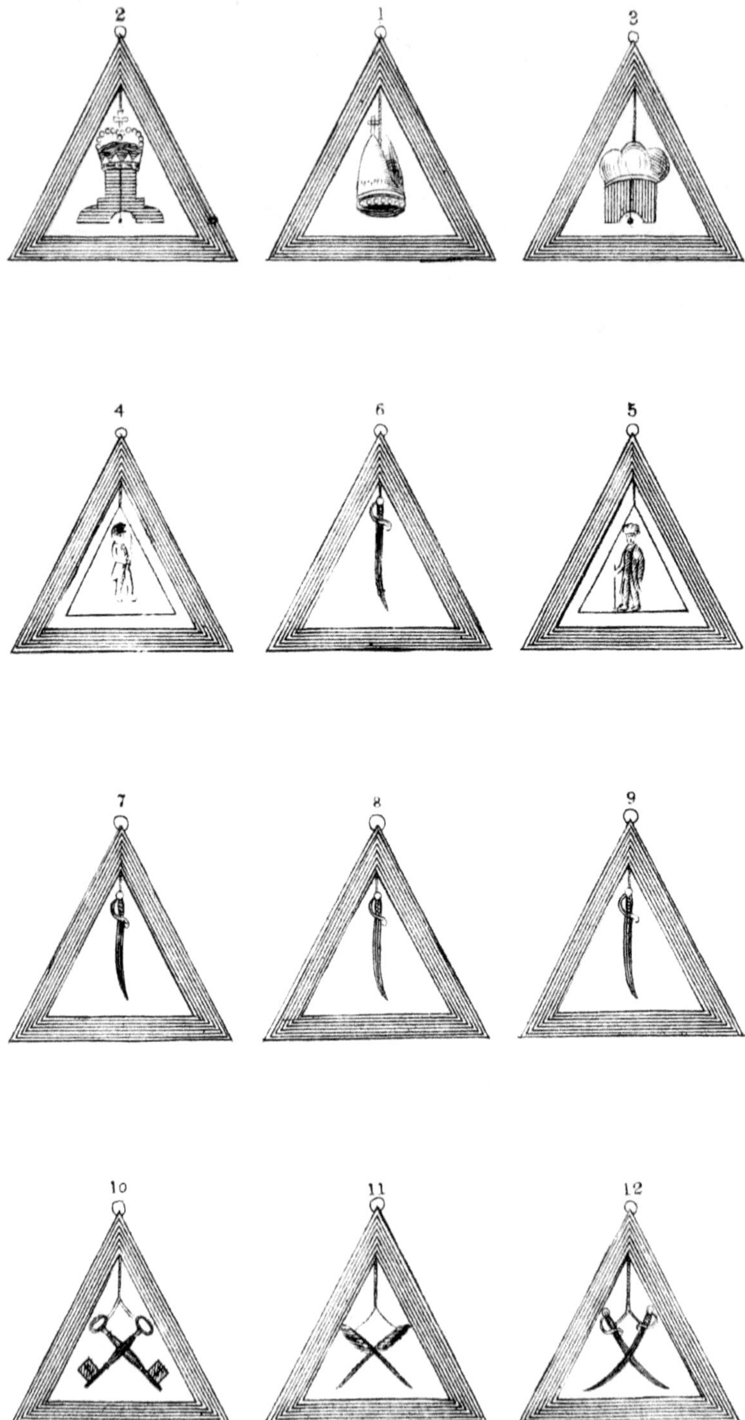
2
1
3
4
6
5
7
8
9
10
11
12

Section Second.

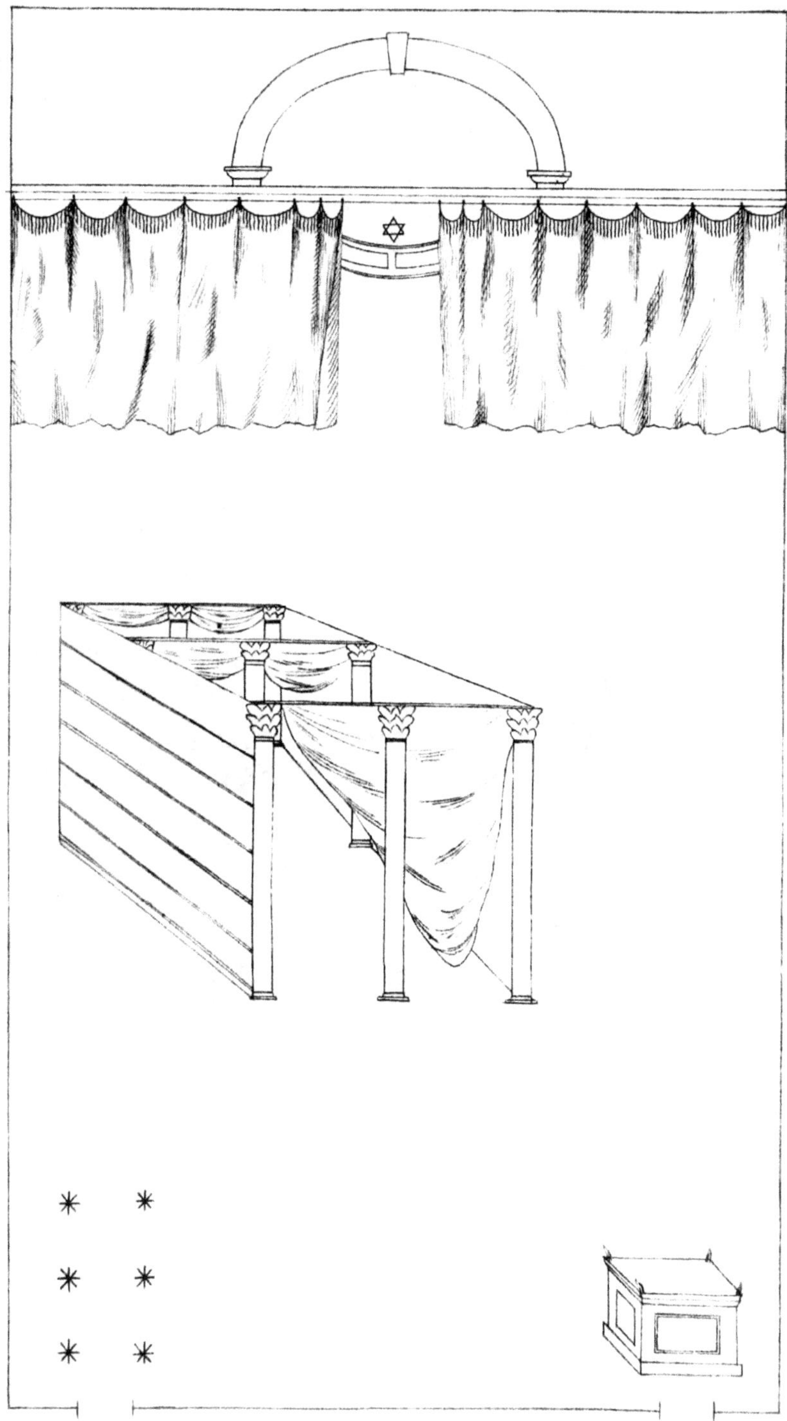

Exodus III.I-II.

DESTRUCTION OF JERUSALEM BY NEBUCHADNEZZAR.

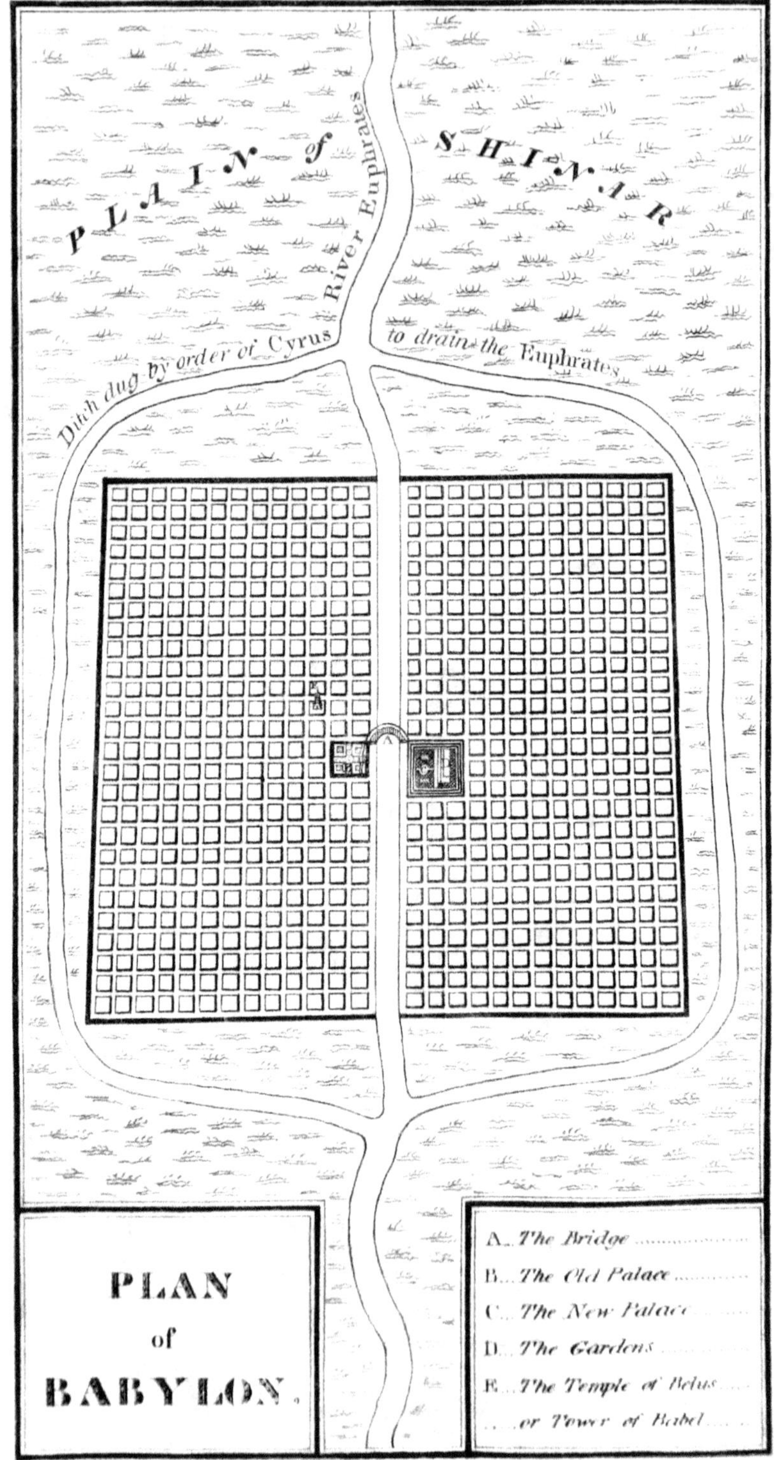
PLAIN of SHINAR
River Euphrates
Ditch dug by order of Cyrus to drain the Euphrates
A
PLAN
of
BABYLON.
A...The Bridge
B...The Old Palace
C...The New Palace
D...The Gardens
E...The Temple of Belus
...or Tower of Babel

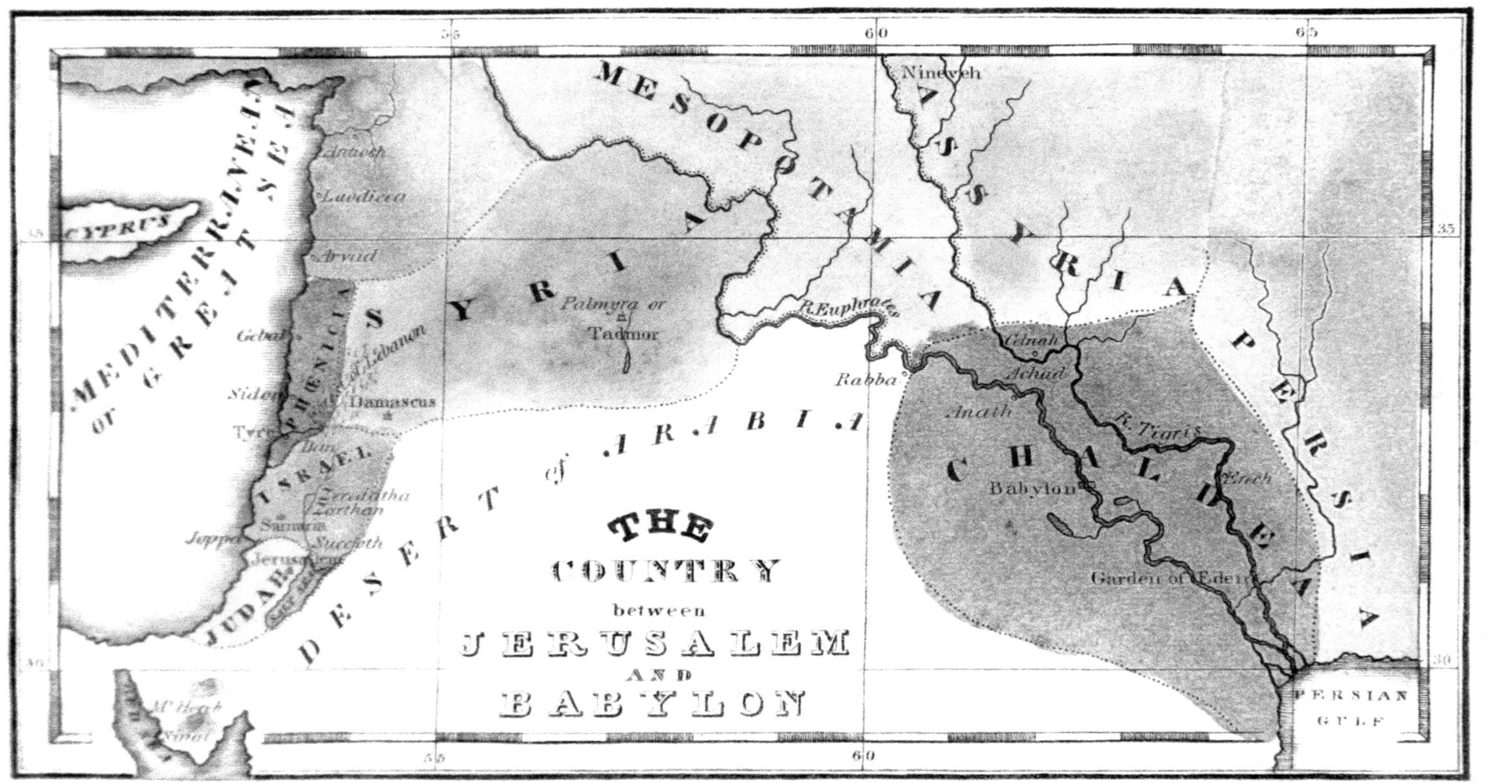
THE
COUNTRY
between
JERUSALEM
AND
BABYLON
MESOPOTAMIA
ASSYRIA
PERSIA
CHALDEA
PERSIAN GULF
SYRIA
DESERT of ARABIA
MEDITERRANEAN or GREAT SEA
CYPRUS
PHOENICIA
ISRAEL
JUDAH
Nineveh
Babylon
Garden of Eden
R. Tigris
R. Euphrates
Palmyra or Tadmor
Damascus
Rabba
Anath
Achad
Calneh
Erech
Antioch
Laodicea
Arvad
Gebal
Sidon
Tyre
Samaria
Joppa
Succoth
Zeredatha
Zarthan
Mt. Sinai
55
60
65
35
30

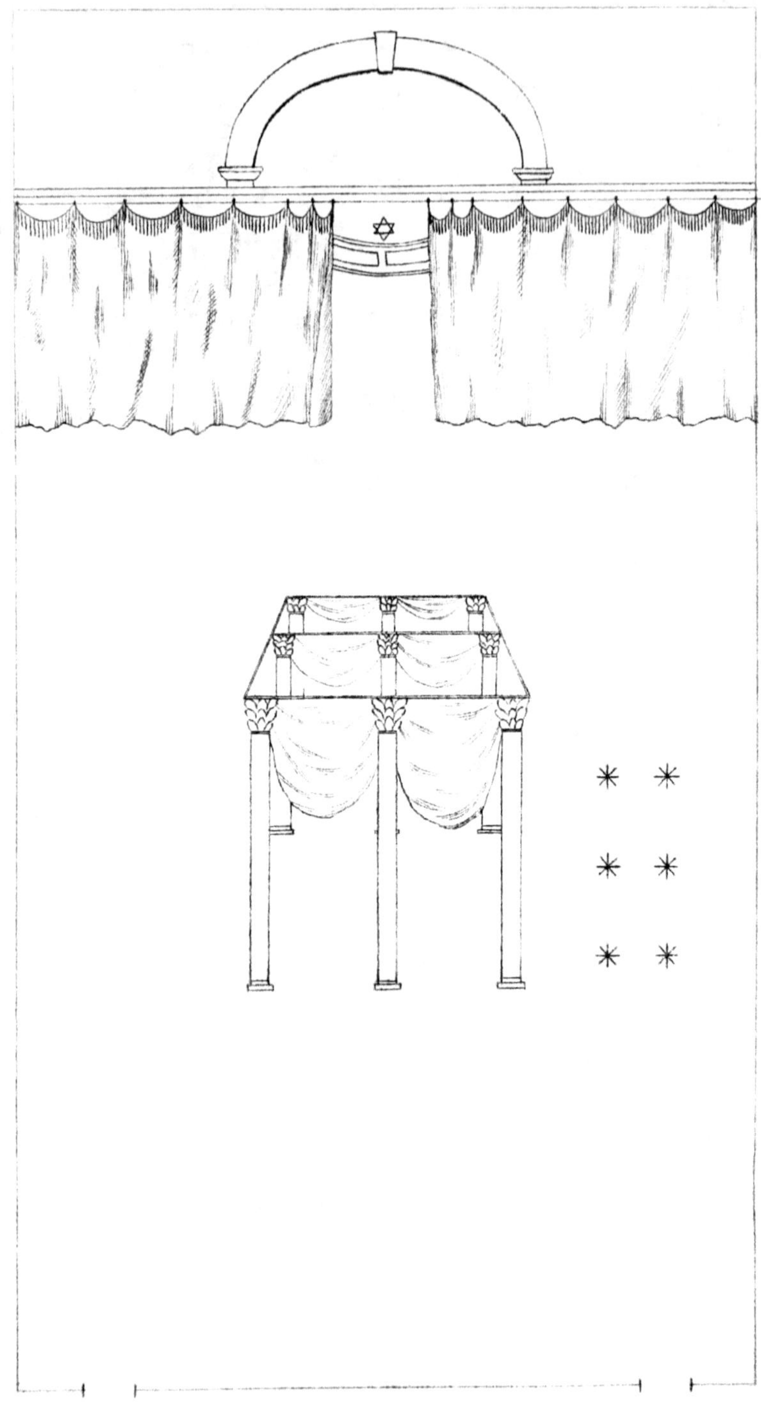

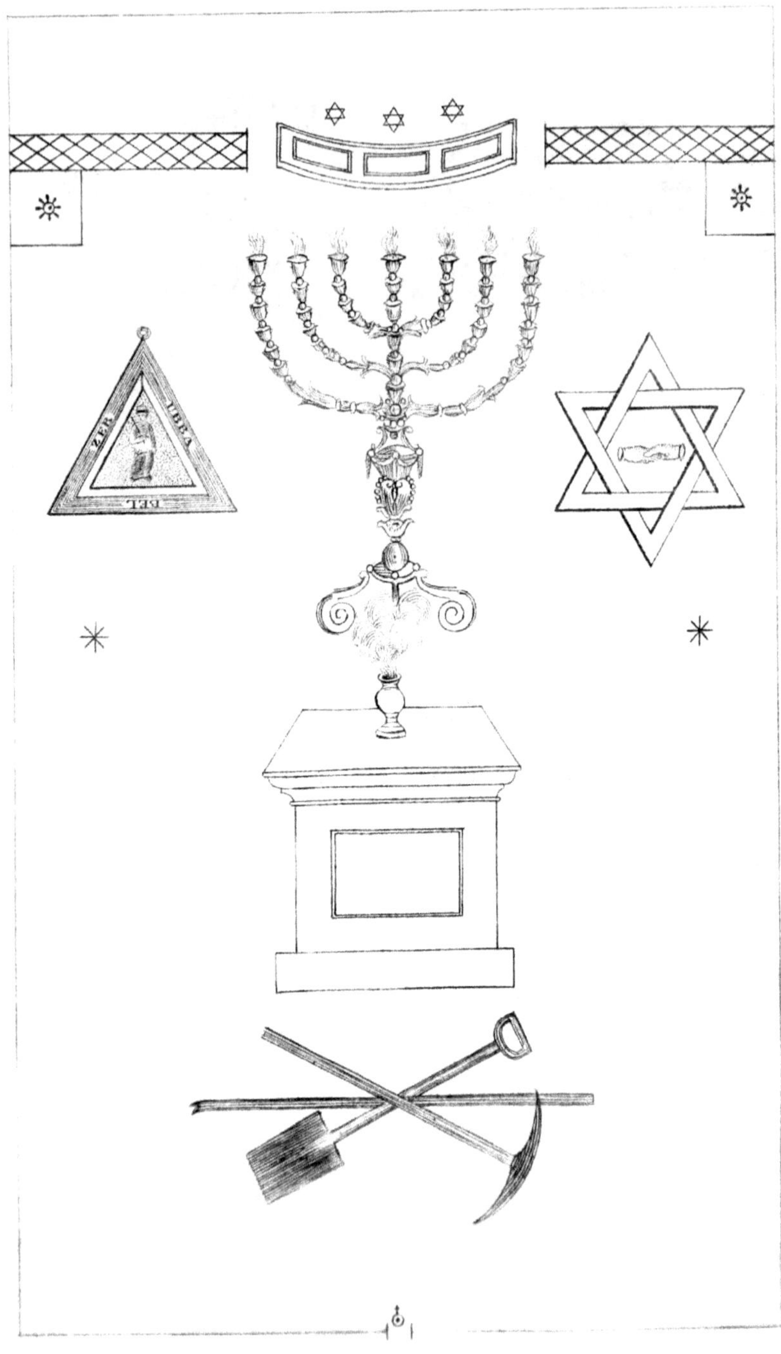
ZER
UBBA
BEL

Ezra V.I-II.

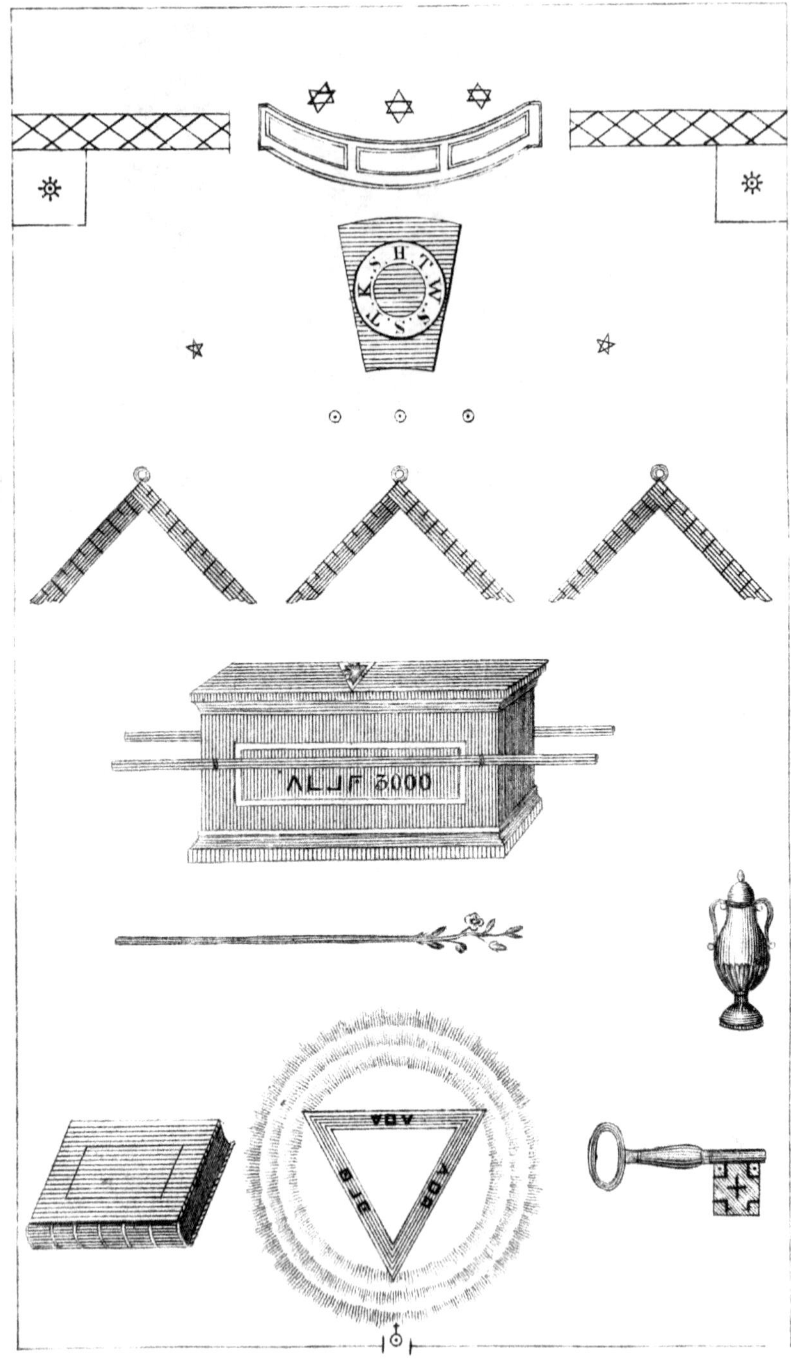
H.T.W.S.S.T.K.S.

ROYAL ARCH MASONRY.
HOLINESS TO THE LORD.

ROYAL MASTERS DEGREE.

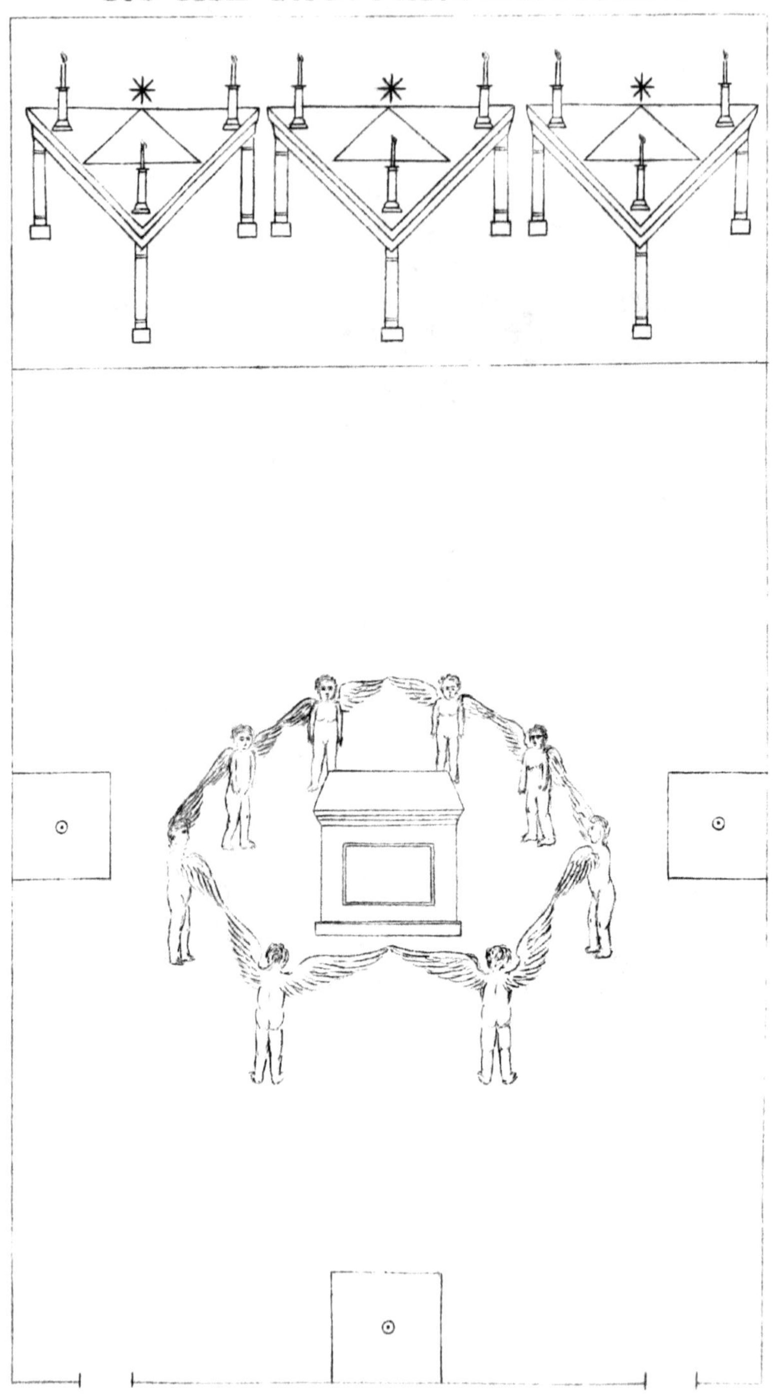

SELECT MASTERS DEGREE.

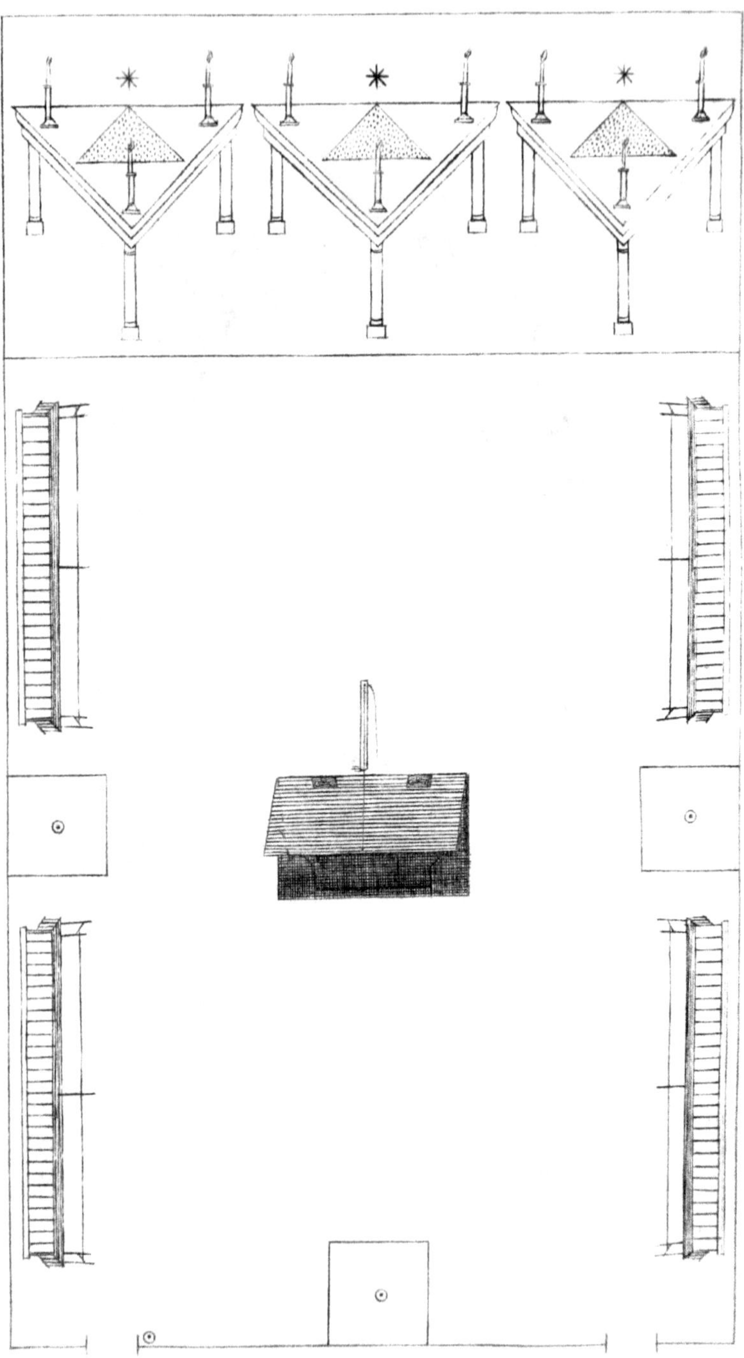

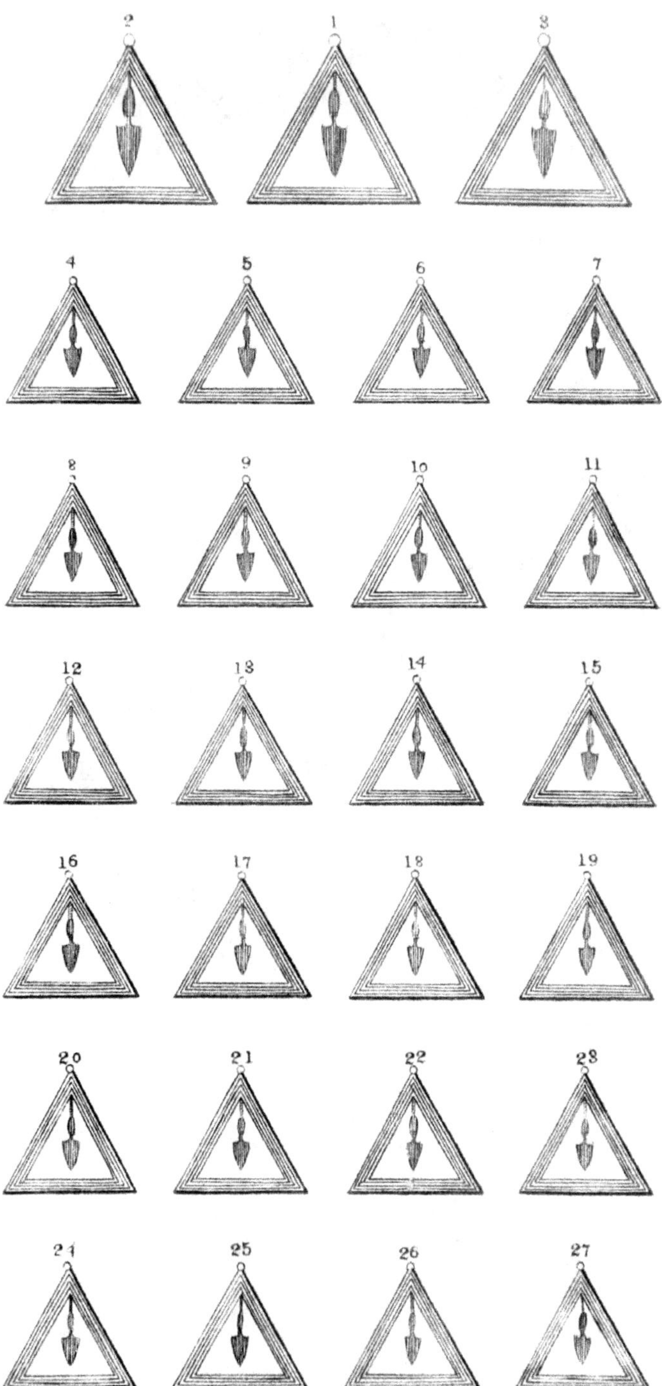
2
1
3
4
5
6
7
8
9
10
11
12
13
14
15
16
17
18
19
20
21
22
23
24
25
26
27

ENTERED APPRENTICE'S DEGREE.

SECTION FIRST.

THE first section consists of general heads; which, though short and simple, carry weight with them, and qualify us to try and examine the rights of others to our privileges, while they prove ourselves. It also accurately elucidates the mode of initiating a candidate into our ancient order.

A Prayer used at the Initiation of a Candidate.

Vouchsafe thine aid, Almighty Father of the universe, to this our present convention; and grant that this candidate for masonry may dedicate and devote his life to thy service, and become a true and faithful brother among us! Endue him with a competency of thy divine Wisdom, that by the secrets of our art he may be better enabled to display the Beauties of Holiness, to the honor of thy holy name! So mote it be. Amen.

The following passage of scripture is rehearsed during the ceremony.

Behold! how good and how pleasant it is for brethren to dwell together in unity:

It is like the precious ointment upon the head, that ran down upon the beard, even Aaron's beard that went down to the skirts of his garment:

As the dew of Hermon, and as the dew that descended upon the mountains of Zion: for there the Lord commanded the blessing, even life for evermore.

Towards the close of the section is explained that peculiar ensign of masonry the *lamb-skin,* or *white leather apron,* which is an emblem of innocence, and the badge of a mason; more ancient than the golden fleece or Roman Eagle; more honorable than the star and garter, or any other order that could be conferred upon the candidate at that or any future period, by king, prince, potentate, or any other person, except he be a mason; and which every one ought to wear with pleasure to himself, and honor to the fraternity.

This section closes with an explanation of the working tools, which are, the *twenty-four inch gauge* and the *common gavel.*

The *twenty-four inch gauge* is an instrument used by operative masons to measure and lay out their work; but we, as free and accepted masons, are taught to make use of it for the more noble and glorious purpose of dividing our time. It being divided into twenty-four equal parts, is emblematical of the twenty-four hours of the day, which we are taught to divide into three equal parts; whereby are found eight hours for the service of God, and a distressed worthy brother; eight for our usual vocations; and eight for refreshment and sleep.

The *common gavel* is an instrument made use of by operative masons to break off the corners of rough stones, the better to fit them for the builder's use; but we, as free and accepted masons, are taught to make use of it for the more noble and glorious purpose of divesting our hearts and consciences of all the vices and superfluities of life; thereby fitting our minds as living stones for that spiritual building, that house not made with hands, eternal in the heavens.

SECTION SECOND.

The second section rationally accounts for the ceremony of initiating a candidate into our ancient institution.

The Badge of a Mason.

Every candidate, at his initiation, is presented with a *lamb-skin,* or *white leather apron.*

The *lamb* has in all ages been deemed an emblem of *innocence:* the lamb-skin is therefore to remind him of that purity of life and conduct, which is so essentially necessary to his gaining admission into the Celestial Lodge above, where the Supreme Architect of the universe presides.

SECTION THIRD.

The third section explains the nature and principles of our Constitution. Here also we receive instructions relative to the *form, supports, covering, furniture, ornaments, lights,* and *jewels* of the Lodge, how it should be *situated,* and to whom *dedicated.*

From East to West, and between North and South, Free-Masonry extends; and in every clime are masons to be found.

Our institution is said to be supported by *Wisdom, Strength,* and *Beauty;* because it is necessary that there should be wisdom to contrive, strength to support, and beauty to adorn, all great and important undertakings.

Its *covering* is no less than a clouded canopy, or a starry-decked Heaven, where all good masons hope at last to arrive, by the aid of the theological ladder, which Jacob, in his vision, saw ascending from earth to heaven; the three *principal rounds* of which are denominated *Faith, Hope,* and *Charity;* and which admonish us to have faith in God, hope in immortality, and charity to all mankind.

The greatest of these is *Charity;* for our Faith may be lost in sight; Hope ends in fruition; but Charity extends beyond the grave, through the boundless realms of eternity.

Every well-governed Lodge is furnished with the *Holy Bible,* the *Square,* and the *Compasses.*

The Holy Bible is dedicated to God; the Square, to the Master; and the Compasses, to the Craft.

The Bible is dedicated to God, because it is the inestimable gift of God to man; *** the square to the master, because it is the proper Masonic emblem of his office; and the compasses to the craft, because, by a due attention to their use, they are taught to circumscribe their desires, and keep their passions within due bounds.

The *Ornaments* of a Lodge, are the *Mosaic pavement,* the *indented tessel,* and the *blazing star.* The *Mosaic pavement* is a representation of the ground floor of King Solomon's temple; the *indented tessel,* that beautiful tessellated border, or skirting, which surrounded it; and the *blazing star* in the centre, is commemorative of the Star which appeared, to guide the wise men of the East to the place of our Savior's nativity.

The *Mosaic pavement* is emblematical of human life, checkered with good and evil; the *beautiful border* which surrounds it, those manifold blessings and comforts which surround us, and which we hope to enjoy by a faithful reliance on Divine Providence, which is hieroglyphically represented by the *blazing star* in the centre.

The *moveable* and *immoveable* Jewels also claim our attention in this section.

The *rough ashler* is a stone as taken from the quarry in its rude and natural state.

The *perfect ashler* is a stone made ready by the hands of the workmen, to be adjusted by the working tools of the Fellow Craft. The *trestle-board* is for the master workman to draw his designs upon.

By the *rough ashler,* we are reminded of our rude and imperfect state by nature; by the *perfect ashler,* that state of perfection at which we hope to arrive by a virtuous education, our own endeavors, and the blessing of God; and by the *trestle-board,* we are also reminded, that as the operative workman erects his temporal building agreeably to the rules and designs laid down by the master, on his trestle-board, so should we, both operative and speculative, Endeavour to erect our spiritual building agreeably to the rules and designs laid down by the Supreme Architect of the universe, in the great Books of nature and revelation, which is our spiritual, moral, and Masonic trestle-board.

Lodges were anciently dedicated to King Solomon, as it is said he was the first Most Excellent Grand Master: Yet masons professing Christianity dedicate theirs to St. John the Baptist, and St. John the Evangelist, who were two eminent Christian patrons of masonry; and since their time, there is represented, in every regular and well-governed Lodge, a certain *point within a circle,** embordered by two perpendicular parallel *lines,* representing St. John the Baptist and St. John the Evangelist; and upon the top rests the Holy Scriptures. In going round this circle, we necessarily touch upon these two lines, as well as the Holy Scriptures; and while a mason keeps himself circumscribed within their precepts, it is impossible that he should materially err.

Of Brotherly Love.

By the exercise of brotherly love, we are taught to regard the whole human species as one family; the high and low, the rich and poor; who, as created by one Almighty Parent, and inhabitants of the same planet, are to aid, support, and protect each other. On this principle, masonry unites men of every country, sect and opinion, and conciliates true friendship

* The *point* represents an individual brother; the *circle* is the boundary line, beyond which he is never to suffer his prejudices or passions to betray him.

among those who might otherwise have remained at a perpetual distance.

Of Relief.

To relieve the distressed, is a duty incumbent on all men; but particularly on masons, who are linked together by an indissoluble chain of sincere affection. To soothe the unhappy; to sympathize with their misfortunes; to compassionate their miseries, and to restore peace to their troubled minds, is the great aim we have in view. On this basis, we form our friendships and establish our connections.

Of Truth.

Truth is a divine attribute, and the foundation of every virtue. To be good and true is the first lesson we are taught in masonry. On this theme we contemplate, and by its dictates Endeavour to regulate our conduct: hence, while influenced by this principle, hypocrisy and deceit are unknown among us; sincerity and plain dealing distinguish us; and the heart and tongue join in promoting each other's welfare, and rejoicing in each other's prosperity.

An Explanation of the four CARDINAL VIRTUES; which are, TEMPERANCE, FORTITUDE, PRUDENCE, and JUSTICE.

Of Temperance.

Temperance is that due restraint upon our affections and passions, which renders the body tame and governable, and frees the mind from the allurements of vice. This virtue should be the constant practice of every mason; as he is thereby taught to avoid excess, or contracting any licentious or vicious habit, the indulgence of which might lead him to disclose some of those valuable secrets, which he has promised to conceal and never reveal, and which would consequently subject him to the contempt and detestation of all good masons.*

* * * *

Of Fortitude.

Fortitude is that noble and steady purpose of the mind, whereby we are enabled to undergo any pain, peril, or danger, when prudentially deemed expedient. This virtue is equally distant from rashness and cowardice; and, like the former, should be deeply impressed upon the mind of every mason, as a safe guard or security against any illegal attack that may be made, by force or otherwise, to extort from him any of those valuable secrets with which he has been so solemnly entrusted, and which were emblematically represented upon his first admission into the Lodge. * * * * *

Of Prudence.

Prudence teaches us to regulate our lives and actions agreeably to the dictates of reason, and is that habit by which we wisely judge, and prudentially determine, on all things relative to our present as well as to our future happiness. This virtue should be the peculiar characteristic of every mason, not only for the government of his conduct while in the Lodge, but also when abroad in the world. It should be particularly attended to, in all strange and mixed companies, never to let fall the least sign, token, or word, whereby the secrets of masonry might be unlawfully obtained. * * * * *

Of Justice.

Justice is that standard, or boundary of right, which enables us to render to every man his just due, without distinction. This virtue is not only consistent with divine and human laws, but is the very cement and support of civil society; and as justice in a great measure constitutes the real good man, so should it be the invariable practice of every mason, never to deviate from the minutest principles thereof. * * * * *

The illustration of these virtues is accompanied with some general observations peculiar to masons. Due veneration is also paid to our ancient patrons.

CHARGE at Initiation into the First Degree. BROTHER,

As you are now introduced into the first principles of masonry, I congratulate you on being accepted into this ancient and honorable order:—ancient, as having subsisted from time immemorial, and honorable, as tending, in every particular, so to render all men who will be conformable to its precepts. No institution was ever raised on a better principle, or more solid foundation; nor were ever more excellent rules and useful maxims laid down, than are inculcated in the several Masonic lectures. The greatest and best of men, in all ages, have been encouragers and promoters of the art; and have never deemed it derogatory to their dignity, to level themselves with the fraternity, extend their privileges, and patronize their assemblies. There are three great duties, which, as a mason, you are charged to inculcate—to God, your neighbor, and yourself. To God, in never mentioning his name, but with that reverential awe which is due from a creature to his Creator; to implore his aid in all your laudable undertakings, and to esteem him as the chief good:—to your neighbor, in acting upon the square, and doing unto him as you wish he should do unto you:—and to yourself, in avoiding all irregularity and intemperance, which may impair your faculties, or debase the dignity of your profession. A zealous attachment to these duties will insure public and private esteem.

In the State, you are to be a quiet and peaceful subject, true to your government, and just to your country; you are not to countenance disloyalty or rebellion, but patiently submit to legal authority, and conform with cheerfulness to the government of the country in which you live. In your outward demeanor, be particularly careful to avoid censure or reproach.

Although your frequent appearance at our regular meetings is earnestly solicited, yet it is not meant that masonry should interfere with your necessary vocations; for these are on no account to be neglected;—neither are you to suffer your zeal for the institution to lead you into argument with those who, through ignorance, may ridicule it.

At your leisure hours that you may improve in Masonic knowledge you are to converse with well informed brethren, who will be always as ready to give, as you will be ready to receive, instruction.

Finally, keep sacred and inviolable the mysteries of the order; as these are to distinguish you from the rest of the community, and mark your consequence among masons. If, in the circle of your acquaintance, you find a person desirous of being initiated into masonry, be particularly attentive not to recommend him, unless you are convinced he will conform to our rules; that the honor, glory, and reputation of the institution, may be firmly established, and the world at large convinced of its good effects.

FELLOW-CRAFT'S DEGREE.

SECTION FIRST.

THE first section recapitulates the ceremony of initiation into this class; and instructs the diligent craftsman how to proceed in the proper arrangement of the ceremonies used on the occasion. It should therefore be well understood by every officer and member of the Lodge.

AMOS 7:7, 8.

"Thus he shewed me; and behold the Lord stood upon a wall made by a plumb-line, with a plumb-line in his hand. And the Lord said unto me, Amos, what seest thou? And I said a plumb-line. Then said the Lord, Behold, I will set a plumb-line in the midst of my people Israel: I will not again pass by them any more."

The working tools of a fellow-craft are here introduced and explained; which are the *plumb, square,* and *level.*

The *plumb* is an instrument made use of by operative masons, to raise perpendiculars; the *square,* to square the work; and the *level,* to lay horizontals; but we, as free and accepted masons, are taught to make use of them for more noble and glorious purposes:

The *plumb* admonishes us to walk uprightly in our several stations before God and man, *squaring* our actions by the square of virtue, and remembering that we are traveling upon the *level* of time, to "that undiscovered country, from who's born no traveler returns."

SECTION SECOND.

The second section of this degree refers to the origin of the institution; and views masonry under two denominations, operative and speculative. The period stipulated for rewarding merit, is here fixed; and the inimitable moral to which that circumstance alludes, is explained. The celestial and terrestrial globes are considered; and here the accomplished mason may display his talents to advantage, in elucidating the *Orders of Architecture,* the *Senses* of human nature, and the liberal *Arts* and *Sciences,* which are severally classed in a regular arrangement.

Masonry is considered under two denominations; operative and speculative.

Operative Masonry.

By operative masonry, we allude to a proper application of the useful rules of architecture, whence a structure will derive figure, strength, and beauty, and whence will result a due proportion and a just correspondence in all its parts. It furnishes us with dwellings, and convenient shelters from the vicissitudes and inclemency of seasons: and while it displays the effects of human wisdom, as well in the choice, as in the arrangement, of the sundry materials of which an edifice is composed, it demonstrates that a fund of science and industry is implanted in man, for the best, most salutary, and beneficent purposes.

Speculative Masonry.

By speculative masonry, we learn to subdue the passions, act upon the square, keep a tongue of good report, maintain secrecy, and practice charity. It is so far interwoven with religion, as to lay us under obligation to pay that rational homage to the Deity, which at once constitutes our duty and our happiness. It leads the contemplative to view, with reverence and admiration, the glorious works of creation, and inspires him with the most exalted ideas of the perfections of his divine Creator.

In six days, God created the heavens and the earth, and rested upon the seventh day;—the seventh, therefore, our ancient brethren consecrated as a day of rest from their labors; thereby enjoying frequent opportunities to contemplate the glorious works of creation, and to adore their great Creator.

Peace, Unity, and Plenty, are here introduced and explained.

The next is the doctrine of the Spheres in the science of Astronomy, introduced and considered.

Of the Globes.

The Globes are two artificial and spherical bodies; on the convex surface of which are represented, the countries, seas, and various parts of the earth, the face of the heavens, the planetary revolutions, and other particulars.

The Use of the Globes.

Their principal use, besides serving as maps to distinguish the outward parts of the earth, and the situation of the fixed stars, is to illustrate and explain the phenomena arising from the annual revolution, and the diurnal rotation, of the earth round its own axis. They are the noblest instruments for improving the mind, and giving it the most distinct idea of any problem or proposition, as well as enabling it to solve the same. Contemplating these bodies, we are inspired with a due reverence for the Deity and his works, and are induced to encourage the studies of astronomy, geography, and navigation, and the arts dependent on them, by which society has been so much benefited.

As the five Orders of Architecture are considered in this section, a brief description of them may not be improper.

Of Order in Architecture.

By order in architecture, is meant a system of all the members, proportions, and ornaments of columns and pilasters;—or, it is a regular arrangement of the projecting parts of a building, which, united with those of a column, form a beautiful, perfect, and complete whole.

Of its Antiquity.

From the first formation of society, order in architecture may be traced. When the rigor of seasons obliged men to contrive shelter from the inclemency of the weather, we learn that they first planted trees on end, and then laid others across, to support a covering. The bands which connected those trees at top and bottom are said to have given rise to the idea of the base and capital of pillars; and from this simple hint originally preceded the more improved art of architecture.

The five Orders are thus classed;—the *Tuscan, Doric, Ionic, Corinthian,* and *Composite.*

The Tuscan

Is the most simple and solid of the five orders. It was invented in Tuscany, whence it derives its name. The simplicity of the construction of this column renders it eligible where ornament would be superfluous.

The Doric,

Which is plain and natural, is the most ancient, and was invented by the Greeks. Its column is eight diameters high, and has seldom any ornaments on base or capital, except moldings; though the frieze is distinguished by triglyphs and metopes; and triglyphs compose the ornaments of the frieze.

The Doric is the best proportioned of all the orders. The several parts, of which it is composed, are founded on the natural position of solid bodies. In its first invention, it was simpler than in its present state. In after times, when it began to be adorned, it gained the name of Doric; for when it was constructed in its primitive and simple form, the name of Tuscan was conferred on it. Hence the Tuscan precedes the Doric in rank, on account of its resemblance to that pillar in its original state.

The Ionic

Bears a kind of mean proportion between the more solid and delicate orders. Its column is nine diameters high; its capital is adorned with volutes, and its cornice has dentals. There is both delicacy and ingenuity displayed in this pillar; the invention of which is attributed to the Ionians, as the famous temple of Diana at Ephesus was of this order. It is said to have been formed after the model of an agreeable young woman, of an elegant shape, dressed in her hair; as a contrast to the Doric order, which was formed after that of a strong, robust man.

The Corinthian,

The richest of the five orders, is deemed a masterpiece of art. Its column is ten diameters high, and its capital is adorned with two rows of leaves, and eight volutes, which sustain the abacus. The frieze is ornamented with curious devices, the cornice with dentals and modillions. This order is used in stately and superb structures.

Of the Invention of this Order.

It was invented at Corinth, by Callimachus, who is said to have taken the hint of the capital of this pillar from the following remarkable circumstance. Accidentally passing by the tomb of a young lady, he perceived a basket of toys upon an acanthus root, covered by a tile. As the branches grew up, they encompassed the basket, till, arriving at the tile, and they met with an obstruction, and bent downwards. Callimachus, struck with the object, set about imitating the figure: the vase of the capital he made to represent the basket; the abacus the tile; and the volutes the bending leaves.

The Composite

Is compounded of the other orders, and was contrived by the Romans. Its capital has the two rows of leaves of the Corinthian, and the volutes of the Ionic. Its column has quarter-rounds, as the Tuscan and Doric order; is ten diameters high; and its cornice has dentals, or simple modillions. This pillar is generally found in buildings where strength, elegance and beauty are displayed.

Of the Invention of Order in Architecture.

The ancient and original orders of architecture revered by masons are no more than three; the Doric, Ionic, and Corinthian, which were invented by the Greeks. To these the Romans have added two; *the Tuscan, which they made plainer than the Doric; and the Composite, which was more ornamental, if not more beautiful, than the Corinthian. The first three orders alone, however, show invention and particular character, and essentially differ from each other: the two others have nothing but what is borrowed, and differ only accidentally: the Tuscan is the Doric in its earliest state: and the Composite is the Corinthian enriched with the Ionic.* To the Greeks, therefore, and not to the Romans, are we indebted for what is great, judicious and distinct, in architecture.

Of the Five Senses of Human Nature, which are, HEARING, SEEING, FEELING, SMELLING, and TASTING.

Hearing

Is that sense by which we distinguish sounds, and are capable of enjoying all the agreeable charms of music. By it we are enabled to enjoy the pleasures of society, and reciprocally to communicate to each other our thoughts and intentions, our purposes and desires; while thus our reason is capable of exerting its utmost power and energy.

The wise and beneficent Author of Nature intended, by the formation of this sense, that we should be social creatures, and receive the greatest and most important part of our knowledge by the information of others. For these purposes, we are endowed with hearing, that by a proper exertion of our rational powers, our happiness may be complete.

Seeing

Is that sense by which we distinguish objects, and in an instant of time, without change of place or situation, view armies in battle array, figures of the stateliest structures, and all the agreeable variety displayed in the landscape of nature. By this sense, we find our way on the pathless ocean, traverse the globe of the earth, determine its figure and dimensions, and delineate any region or quarter of it. By it we measure the planetary orbs, and make new discoveries in the sphere of the fixed stars. Nay, more: by it we perceive the tempers and dispositions, the passions and affections, of our fellow-creatures, when they wish most to conceal them; so that though the tongue may be taught to lie and dissemble, the countenance would display the hypocrisy to the discerning eye. In fine, the rays of light, which administer to this sense, are the most astonishing part of the animated creation, and render the eye a peculiar object of admiration.

Of all the faculties, sight is the noblest. The structure of the eye, and its appurtenances, evince the admirable contrivance of nature for performing all its various external and internal motions; while the variety displayed in the eyes of different animals, suited to their several ways of life, clearly demonstrates this organ to be the master-piece of Nature's work.

Feeling

Is that sense by which we distinguish the different qualities of bodies: such as heat and cold, hardness, and softness, roughness, and smoothness, figure, solidity, motion, and extension.

These three senses, Hearing, Seeing, and Feeling, are most revered among masons.

Smelling

Is that sense, by which we distinguish odors, the various kinds of which convey different impressions to the mind. Animal and vegetable bodies, and indeed most other bodies, while exposed to the air, continually send forth effluvia of vast subtlety, as well in the state of life and growth, as in the state of fermentation and putrefaction. These effluvia being drawn into the nostrils along with the air are the means by which all bodies are smelled. Hence it is evident that there is a manifest appearance of design in the great Creator's having planted the organ of smell in the inside of that canal, through which the air continually passes in respiration.

Tasting

Enables us to make a proper distinction in the choice of our food. The organ of this sense guards the entrance of the alimentary canal, as that of smelling guards the entrance of the canal for respiration. From the situation of both these organs, it is plain that they were intended by nature to distinguish wholesome food from that which is nauseous. Every thing that enters into the stomach must undergo the scrutiny of tasting; and by it we are capable of discerning the changes which the same body undergoes in the different compositions of art, cookery, chemistry, pharmacy, &c.

Smelling and tasting are inseparably connected; and it is by the unnatural kind of life men commonly lead in society, that these senses are rendered less fit to perform their natural offices.

Of the Seven Liberal Arts and Sciences;—which are, GRAMMAR, RHETORIC, LOGIC, ARITHMETIC, GEOMETRY, MUSIC, and ASTRONOMY.

Grammar

Teaches the proper arrangement of words, according to the idiom or dialect of any particular people; and that Excellencies of pronunciation, which enables us to speak or write a language with accuracy, agreeably to reason and correct usage.

Rhetoric

Teaches us to speak copiously and fluently on any subject, not merely with propriety alone, but with all the advantages of force and elegance, wisely contriving to captivate the hearer by strength of argument and beauty of expression, whether it be to entreat or exhort, to admonish or applaud.

Logic

Teaches us to guide our reason discretionally in the general knowledge of things, and directs our inquiries after truth. It consists of a regular train of argument, whence we infer, deduce and conclude, according to certain premises laid down, admitted, or granted; and in it are employed the faculties of conceiving, judging, reasoning and disposing; all of which are naturally led on from one gradation to another, till the point in question is finally determined.

Arithmetic

Teaches the powers and properties of numbers, which is variously effected, by letters, tables, figures, and instruments. By this art, reasons and demonstrations are given, for finding out any certain number, whose relation or affinity to another is already known or discovered.

Geometry.

Geometry treats of the powers and properties of magnitudes in general, where length, breadth, and thickness, are considered, from a point to a line, from a line to a superficies, and from a superficies to a solid.

A point is a dimensionless figure; or an indivisible part of a space.

A line is a point continued, and a figure of one capacity, namely, length.

A superficies is a figure of two dimensions, namely, length, and breadth.

A solid is a figure of three dimensions, namely, length, breadth, and thickness.

Of the Advantages of Geometry.

By this science, the architect is enabled to construct his plans, and execute his designs; the general to arrange his soldiers; the geographer to give us the dimensions of the world, and all things therein contained; to delineate the extent of seas, and specify the divisions of empires, kingdoms and provinces. By it, also, the astronomer is enabled to make his observations, and to fix the duration of time and seasons, years and cycles.

In fine, geometry is the foundation of architecture, and the root of the mathematics.

Music

Teaches the art of forming concords, so as to compose delightful harmony, by a mathematical and proportional arrangement of acute, grave, and mixed sounds. This art, by a series of experiments, is reduced to a demonstrative science, with respect to tones and the intervals of sound. It inquires into the nature of concords and discords, and enables us to find out the proportion between them by numbers.

Astronomy

Is that divine art, by which we are taught to read the wisdom, strength and beauty, of the Almighty Creator, in those sacred pages, the celestial hemisphere.

Assisted by astronomy, we can observe the magnitudes, and calculate the periods and eclipses of the heavenly bodies. By it, we learn the use of globes, the system of the world, and the preliminary law of nature. While we are employed in the study of this science, we must perceive unparalleled instances of wisdom and goodness; and, through the whole creation, trace the glorious Author by his works.

[Here an emblem of Plenty is introduced and explained.]

Of the Moral Advantages of Geometry.

Geometry, the first and noblest of sciences, is the basis on which the superstructure of masonry is erected. By geometry, we may curiously trace Nature through her various windings, to her most concealed recesses. By it, we may discover the power, the wisdom and the goodness of the Grand Artificer of the universe, and view with delight the proportions which connect this vast machine.

By it, we may discover how the planets move in their different orbits, and demonstrate their various revolutions. By it we account for the return of seasons, and the variety of scenes which each season displays to the discerning eye. Numberless worlds are around us, all framed by the same Divine Artist, which roll through the vast expanse, and are all conducted by the same unerring law of nature.

A survey of Nature, and the observations of her beautiful proportions, first determined man to imitate the divine plan, and study symmetry and order. This gave rise to societies, and birth to every useful art. The architect began to design; and the plans which he laid down, being improved by experience and time, have produced works which are the admiration of every age.

The lapse of time, the ruthless hand of ignorance, and the devastations of war, have laid waste and destroyed many valuable monuments of antiquity; on which the utmost exertions of human genius have been employed. Even the temple of Solomon, so spacious and magnificent, and constructed by so many celebrated artists, escaped not the unsparing ravages of barbarous force. Free-Masonry, notwithstanding, has still survived. The *attentive Ear* receives the sound from the *instructive Tongue*: and the mysteries of free-masonry are safely lodged in the repository of *faithful Breasts.* Tools and instruments of architecture, and symbolic emblems, most expressive, are selected by the fraternity, to imprint on the mind wise and serious truths; and thus, through a succession of ages, are transmitted, unimpaired, the most excellent tenets of our institution.

CHARGE at passing to the Degree of Fellow Craft.

BROTHER—

Being passed to the second degree of masonry, we congratulate yon on your preferment. The internal, and not the external qualifications of a man, are what masonry regards. As you increase in knowledge, you will improve in social intercourse.

It is unnecessary to recapitulate the duties which, as a mason, you are bound to discharge, or to enlarge on the necessity of a strict adherence to them, as your own experience must have established their value. Our laws and regulations you are strenuously to support; and be always ready to assist in seeing them duly executed. You are not to palliate, or aggravate, the offences of your brethren; but in the decision of every trespass against our rules, you are to judge with candor admonish with friendship, and reprehend with justice.

The study of the liberal arts, that valuable branch of education, which tends so effectually to polish and adorn the mind, is earnestly recommended to your consideration; especially the science of geometry, which is established as the basis of our art. Geometry, or masonry, originally synonymous terms, being of a divine and moral nature, is enriched with the most useful knowledge: while it proves the wonderful properties of nature, it demonstrates the more important truths of morality.

Your past behavior and regular deportment have merited the honor which we have now conferred; and in your new character, it is expected that you will conform to the principles of the order, by steadily persevering in the practice of every commendable virtue. Such is the nature of your engagement as a fellow craft, and to these duties you are bound by the most sacred ties.

MASTER MASON'S DEGREE.

SECTION FIRST.

THE ceremony of rising to the sublime degree of Master Mason is particularly specified, and other useful instructions are given in this branch of the lecture.

The following passage of scripture is introduced during the ceremonies:

ECCL. 12:1-7.

"Remember now thy Creator in the days of thy youth, while the evil days come not, nor the years draw nigh, when thou shalt say, I have no pleasure in them; while the sun, or the light, or the moon, or the stars, be not darkened, nor the clouds return after the rain; in the day when the keepers of the house shall tremble, and the strong men shall bow themselves, and the grinders cease because they are few, and those that look out of the windows be darkened; and the doors shall be shut in the streets, when the sound of the grinding is low; and he shall rise up at the voice of the bird, and all the daughters of music shall be brought low. Also, when they shall be afraid of that which is high, and fears shall be in the way, and the almond-tree shall flourish, and the grasshopper shall be a burden, and desire shall fail; because man goeth to his long home, and the mourners go about the streets: or ever the silver cord be loosed, or the golden bowl be broken at the fountain, or the wheel broken at the cistern. Then shall the dust return to the earth as it was; and the spirit shall return unto God who gave it"

The *working tools* of a master mason are all the implements of masonry indiscriminately, but more especially *the trowel.*

The TROWEL is an instrument made use of by operative masons, to spread the cement which unites a building into one common mass: but we, as free and accepted masons, are taught to make use of it for the more noble and glorious purpose of spreading the cement of BROTHERLY LOVE and affection; that cement which unites us into one sacred band, or society of friends and brothers, among whom no contention should ever exist, but that noble contention, or rather emulation, of who can best work, or best agree.

SECTION SECOND.

This section recites the historical traditions of the order, and presents to view a finished picture, of the utmost consequence to the fraternity. It exemplifies an instance of virtue, fortitude, and integrity, unparalleled in the history of man.

Prayer at raising a Brother to the sublime Degree of Master Mason.

Thou, O God! knowest our down-sitting and our up-rising, and understandest our thoughts afar off. Shield and defend us from the evil intentions of our enemies, and support us under the trials and afflictions we are destined to endure, while traveling through this vale of tears. Man that is born of a woman is of few days, and full of trouble. He cometh forth as a flower, and is cut down; he fleeth also as a shadow, and continueth not. Seeing his days are determined, the number of his months are with thee, thou hast appointed his bounds that he cannot pass: turn from him that he may rest, till he shall accomplish his day. For there is hope of a tree, if it be cut down, that it will sprout again, and that the tender branch thereof will not cease. But man dieth and wasteth away; yea, man giveth up the ghost, and where is he? As the waters fail from the sea, and the flood decayeth and drieth up, so man lieth down, and riseth not up till the heavens shall be no more. Yet, O Lord! have compassion on the children of thy creation; administer them comfort in time of trouble, and save them with an everlasting salvation.

So mote it be. Amen.

SECTION THIRD.

The third section illustrates certain hieroglyphical emblems, and inculcates many useful lessons, to extend knowledge, and promote virtue. In this branch of the lecture, many particulars relative to King Solomon's Temple are noticed.

This famous fabric was supported by fourteen hundred and fifty-three columns, and two thousand nine hundred and six pilasters; all hewn from the finest Parian marble. There were employed in its building, three Grand Masters; three thousand three hundred overseers of the work; eighty thousand Fellow Crafts, or hewers on the mountains and in the quarries; and seventy thousand Entered Apprentices, or bearers of burdens.

The Three Steps,

Usually delineated upon the master's carpet, are emblematical of the three principal stages of human life, viz. *youth, manhood,* and *age.* In *youth,* as entered apprentices, we ought industriously to occupy our minds in the attainment of useful knowledge: in *manhood,* as fellow crafts, we should apply our knowledge to the discharge of our respective duties to God, our neighbors, and ourselves; that so, in *age,* as master masons, we may enjoy the happy reflections consequent on a well-spent life, and die in the hope of a glorious immortality.

The Pot of Incense

Is an emblem of a pure heart, which is always an acceptable sacrifice to the Deity; and, as this glows with fervent heat, so should our hearts continually glow with gratitude to the great beneficent Author of our existence, for the manifold blessings and comforts we enjoy.

The Bee Hive

Is an emblem of industry, and recommends the practice of that virtue to all created beings, from the highest seraph in heaven, to the lowest reptile of the dust. It teaches us that as we came into the world rational and intelligent beings, so we should ever be industrious ones; never sitting down contented while our fellow-creatures around us are in want, when it is in our power to relieve them, without inconvenience to ourselves.

When we take a survey of nature, we view man, in his infancy, more helpless and indigent than the brutal creation: he lies languishing for days, months, and years, totally incapable of providing sustenance for himself, of guarding against the attack of the wild beasts of the field, or sheltering himself from the inclemency of the weather. It might have pleased the Great Creator of heaven and earth, to have made man independent of all other beings; but, as dependence is one of the strongest bonds of society, mankind were made dependent on each other for protection and security, as they thereby enjoy better opportunities of fulfilling the duties of reciprocal love and friendship. Thus was man formed for social and active life, the noblest part of the work of God; and he that will so demean himself, as not to be endeavoring to add to the common stock of knowledge and understanding, may be deemed a *drone* in the *hive* of nature, a useless member of society, and unworthy of our protection as masons.

The Book of Constitutions, guarded by the Tyler's Sword,

Reminds us that we should be ever watchful and guarded in our words and actions, particularly when before the enemies of masonry; ever bearing in remembrance those truly Masonic virtues, *silence* and *circumspection.*

The Sword, pointing to a Naked Heart,

Demonstrates that justice will sooner or later overtake us; and although our thoughts, words and actions, may be hidden from the eyes of men, yet that

ALL-SEEING EYE,

Whom the SUN, MOON, and STARS obey, and under whose watchful care even COMETS perform their stupendous revolutions, pervades the inmost recesses of the human HEART, and will reward us according to our merits.

The Anchor and Ark

Are emblems of a well-grounded *hope,* and a well spent life. They are emblematical of that divine *Ark,* which safely wafts us over this tempestuous sea of troubles, and that *Anchor* which shall safely moor us in a peaceful harbor, where the wicked cease from troubling, and the weary shall find rest.

The Forty-Seventh Problem of Euclid.

This was an invention of our ancient friend and brother, the great Pythagoras, who, in his travels through Asia, Africa, and Europe, was initiated into several orders of priesthood, and raised to the sublime degree of a master mason. This wise philosopher enriched his mind abundantly in a general knowledge of things, and more especially in geometry, or masonry. On this subject, he drew out many problems and theorems; and among the most distinguished, he erected this, which, in the joy of his heart, he called *Ευρηκα, (Eureka,)* in the Grecian language, signifying *I have found it;* and upon the discovery of which, he is said to have sacrificed a hecatomb. It teaches masons to be general lovers of the arts and sciences.

The Hour-Glass

Is an emblem of human life. Behold! How swiftly the sands run, and how rapidly our lives are drawing to a close! We cannot without astonishment behold the little particles which are contained in this machine;—how they pass away almost imperceptibly! And yet, to our surprise, in the short space of an hour, they are all exhausted. Thus wastes man! To-day, he puts forth the tender leaves of hope; to-morrow, blossoms, and bears his blushing honors thick upon him; the next day comes a frost, which nips the shoot; and when he thinks his greatness is still aspiring, he falls, like autumn leaves, to enrich our mother earth.

The Scythe

Is an emblem of time, which cuts the brittle thread of life, and launches us into eternity.—Behold! What havoc the scythe of time makes among the human race!

If by chance we should escape the numerous evils incident to childhood and youth, and with health and vigor arrive to the years of manhood; yet, withal, we must soon be cut down by the all-devouring scythe of time, and be gathered into the land where our fathers have gone before us.

Thus we close the explanation of the emblems upon the solemn thought of death, which, without revelation, is dark and gloomy; but the Christian is suddenly revived by the *ever green* and ever living *sprig* of Faith in the merits of the Lion of the tribe of Judah; which strengthens him, with confidence and composure, to look forward to a blessed immortality; and doubts not, but in the glorious morn of the resurrection, his body will rise, and become as incorruptible as his soul.

Then let us imitate the Christian in his virtuous and amiable conduct; in his unfeigned piety to God; in his inflexible fidelity to his trust; that we may welcome the grim tyrant Death, and receive him as a kind messenger sent from our Supreme Grand Master, to translate us from this imperfect to that all-perfect, glorious, and celestial Lodge above, where the Supreme Architect of the universe presides.

CHARGE at raising to the sublime degree of Master Mason.

BROTHER,

Your zeal for the institution of masonry; the progress you have made in the mystery; and your conformity to our regulations, have pointed you out as a proper object of our favor and esteem. You are now bound by duty, honor and gratitude, to be faithful to your trust; to support the dignity of your character on every occasion; and to enforce, by precept and example, obedience to the tenets of the order.

In the character of a master mason, you are authorized

to correct the errors and irregularities of your uninformed brethren, and to guard them against a breach of fidelity. To preserve the reputation of the fraternity unsullied, must be your constant care; and for this purpose, it is your province to recommend to your inferiors, obedience and submission; to your equals, courtesy and affability; to your superiors, kindness and condescension. Universal benevolence you are always to inculcate; and, by the regularity of your own behavior, afford the best example for the conduct of others less informed. The ancient land-marks of the order, entrusted to your care, you are carefully to preserve; and never suffer them to be infringed, or countenance a deviation from the established usages and customs of the fraternity.

Your virtue, honor and reputation, are concerned in supporting with dignity the character you now bear. Let no motive, therefore, make you swerve from your duty, violate your vows, or betray your trust; but be true and faithful, and imitate the example of that celebrated artist, whom you this evening represent. Thus you will render yourself deserving of the honor which we have conferred, and merit the confidence that we have reposed.

MARK MASTER'S DEGREE.

BY the influence of this degree, each operative mason, at the erection of King Solomon's temple, was known and distinguished, by the Senior Grand Warden. If defects were found, the overseers were enabled, without difficulty, to ascertain who was the faulty workman: so that deficiencies might be remedied, without injuring the credit or diminishing the reward of the industrious and faithful of the craft.

CHARGE to be read at Opening.

"Wherefore, brethren, lay aside all malice, and guile, and hypocrisies, and envies, and all evil speaking. If so be ye have tasted that the Lord is gracious; to whom coming, as unto a living stone, disallowed indeed of men, but chosen of God, and precious; ye also, as living stones, be ye built up a spiritual house, an holy priesthood, to offer up sacrifices acceptable to God.

"Brethren, this is the will of God, that with well-doing, ye put to silence the ignorance of foolish men. As free, and not as using your liberty for a cloak of maliciousness; but as the servants of God. Honor all men; love the brotherhood; fear God."

SECTION FIRST.

The first section explains the manner of opening a Mark Master's Lodge; and recapitulates the mystic ceremony of the preparatory circumstance of introducing a candidate. The number of artists employed in building the Temple is specified; and the progress they made in architecture is remarked; and it ends with a beautiful display of the manner in which one of the principal events originated, which characterizes this degree.

SECTION SECOND.

In the second section is recited the mode of advancing a candidate to this degree—By which the mark master is instructed in the origin and history of the Degree, and in the indispensable obligations he is under to stretch forth his assisting hand for the relief of an indigent and worthy brother, to a certain specified extent. We are here taught to ascribe praise to the meritorious, and to dispense rewards to the diligent and industrious.

The following texts of scripture are introduced and explained.

PSALM 118:22.

"The stone which the builders refused, is become the head stone of the corner."——MATT. 21:42. "Did ye never read in the scriptures, The stone which the builders rejected, is become the head of the corner?"——MARK 12:10. "And have you not read this scripture, The stone which the builders rejected, is become the head of the corner?"——LUKE 20:17. "What is this, then, that is written, The stone which the builders rejected, is become the head of the corner."

ACTS 4:11.

"This is the stone which was set at naught of you, builders, which is become the head of the corner."

REV. OF ST. JOHN 2:17.

"To him that overcomes, will I give to eat of the hidden manna; and I will give him a *white stone,* and in the stone a *new name* written, which no man Chynoweth, saving him that received it."

REV. III. 13.

"He that hath *an ear* to hear let him hear."

2 CHIRON. 2:16.

"And we will cut wood out of Lebanon, as much as thou salt need; and we will bring it to thee in floats by sea to Joppa, and thou salt carry it up to Jerusalem."

EZEKIEL 44:1, 5.

"Then he brought me back the way of the gate of the outward sanctuary, which looked towards the east, and it was shut. And the Lord said unto me, Son of man, mark well, and behold with thane eyes, and hear with thane ears, all that I say unto thee, concerning all the ordinances of the house of the Lord, and all the laws thereof; and mark well the entering in of the house, with every going forth of the sanctuary."

The *working tools* of a mark master, are the chisel and mallet.

The Chisel

Morally demonstrates the advantages of discipline and education. The mind, like the diamond in its original state, is rude and unpolished; but as the effect of the chisel on the external coat soon presents to view the latent beauties of the diamond; so education discovers the latent virtues of the mind, and draws them forth to range the large field of matter and space, to display the summit of human knowledge, our duty to God and to man.

The Mallet

Morally teaches to correct irregularities, and to reduce man to a proper level; so that, by quiet deportment, he may, in the school of discipline, learn to be content.—What the mallet is to the workman, enlightened reason is to the passions: it curbs ambition, it depresses envy, it moderates anger, and it encourages good dispositions; whence arises among good masons that comely order,

"Which nothing earthly gives, or can destroy,
"The soul's calm sunshine, and the heart-felt joy."

CHARGE to be delivered when a candidate is advanced to the degree of Mark Master.

BROTHER,

I congratulate you on having been thought worthy of being advanced to this honorable degree of masonry. Permit me to impress it on your mind, that your assiduity should ever be commensurate with your duties, which become more and more extensive, as you advance in masonry.

In the honorable character of mark master mason, it is more particularly your duty to Endeavour to let your conduct in the lodge, and among your brethren, be such as may stand the test of the Grand Overseer's square; that you may not, like the unfinished and imperfect work of the negligent and unfaithful of former times, be rejected and thrown aside, as unfit for that spiritual building, that house not made with hands, eternal in the heavens.

While such is your conduct, should misfortunes assail you, should friends forsake you, should envy traduce your good name, and malice persecute you; yet may you have confidence, that among mark master masons you will find friends who will administer relief to your distresses, and comfort your afflictions; ever bearing in mind, as a consolation under all the frowns of fortune, and as an encouragement to hope for better prospects, that *the stone which the builders rejected,* [possessing merits to them unknown,] became the chief stone of the corner.

The following Song is sung previous to closing.

MARK MASTER'S SONG.

You who have pass'd the square,
For your rewards prepare,
Join heart and hand;
Each with his mark in view,
March with the just and true;
Wages to you are due,
At your command.

Hiram, the widow's son,
Sent unto Solomon
Our great key-stone;
On it appears the name
Which raises high the fame
Of all to whom the same
Is truly known.

Now to the westward move,
Where, full of strength and love,
Hiram doth stand;
But if impostors are
Mix'd with the worthy there,
Caution them to beware
Of the right hand.

Now to the praise of those
Who triumph'd o'er the foes
Of mason's art;

To the praiseworthy three,
Who founded this degree;
May all their virtues be
Deep in our hearts.

Previous to closing, the following Parable is recited.

MATTHEW 20:1-16.

"For the kingdom of heaven is like unto a man that is an householder, which went out early in the morning to hire laborers into his vineyard. And when he had agreed with the labourers for a penny a day, he sent them into his vineyard. And he went out about the third hour, and saw others standing idle in the market place, and said unto them, Go ye also into the vineyard, and whatsoever is right, I will give you.—And they went their way. And again he went out about the sixth and ninth hour, and did likewise. And about the eleventh hour, he went out and found others standing idle, and saith unto them, Why stand ye here all the day idle? They say unto him, Because no man hath hired us. He saith unto them, Go ye also into the vineyard, and whatsoever is right, that shall ye receive. So, when even was come, the lord of the vineyard saith unto his steward, Call the labourers, and give them their hire, beginning from the last unto the first. And when they came, that were hired about the eleventh hour, they received every man a penny. But when the first came, they supposed that they should have received more, and they likewise received every man a penny. And when they received it, they murmured against the good man of the house, saying, These last have wrought but one hour, and thou hast made them equal unto us, which have borne the burden and heat of the day. But he answered one of them, and said, Friend, I do thee no wrong; didst thou not agree with me for a penny? Take that thine is, and go thy way; I will give unto this last even as unto thee. Is it not lawful for me to do what I will with my own? Is thine eye evil, because I am good? So the last shall be first, and the first last: for many be called, but few chosen."

PRESENT, OR PAST MASTER'S DEGREE.

THIS degree treats of the government of our society; the disposition of our rulers; and illustrates their requisite qualifications. It includes the ceremony of opening and closing lodges in the several preceding degrees: it comprehends the ceremonies and forms of installations, consecrations, laying the foundation stones of public buildings, and also at dedications and at funerals, by a variety of particulars explanatory of those ceremonies.

SECTION FIRST.

This section contains the form of a petition for letters of dispensation, or a warrant of constitution for a lodge, empowering them to work. The ceremonies of Constitution and Consecration are considered, with the form of a Grand Procession.

Form of Petition for a Charter or Warrant to establish a new Lodge.

To the Most Worshipful Grand Lodge of the State of—
——, the petitioners hereof humbly show, that they are *ancient, free, and accepted Master Masons.* Having the prosperity of the Fraternity at heart, they are willing to exert their best endeavors to promote and diffuse the genuine principles of Masonry.

For the convenience of their respective dwellings, and for other good reasons, they are desirous of forming a new Lodge in the town of ——, to be named ——. In consequence of this desire, and for the good of the craft, they pray for a *Charter,* or *Warrant,* to empower them to assemble as a legal Lodge, to discharge the duties of masonry, in the several degrees of Entered Apprentice, Fellow-Craft, and Master Mason, in a regular and constitutional manner, according to the ancient form of the fraternity, and the laws and regulations of the Grand Lodge. That they have nominated and do recommend A. B. to be the first master, C. D. to be the first senior warden, and E. F. to be the first junior warden of said Lodge: that, if the prayer of the petition should be granted, they promise a strict conformity to all the constitutional laws, rules and regulations of the Grand Lodge.

This petition must be signed by at least seven regular masons, and recommended by some lodge contiguous to the place where the new lodge is to be held. It must be delivered to the Grand Secretary, whose duty it is to lay it before the Grand Lodge.

After a charter is granted by the Grand Lodge, the Grand Master appoints a day and hour for constituting and consecrating the new lodge, and for installing the master, wardens, and other officers. The Grand Master has power to appoint some worthy *Past Master,* with full power to consecrate, constitute, and install the petitioners.

Ceremony of Constitution and Consecration.

On the day and hour appointed, the Grand Master and his officers meet in a convenient room near to the Lodge to be constituted, and open in the third degree.

After the officers in the new lodge are examined, they send a messenger to the Grand Master, with the following message: viz.

MOST WORSHIPFUL,

The officers and brethren of ——— Lodge, who are now assembled at ———, have instructed me to inform you, that the Most Worshipful Grand Lodge was pleased to grant them a Charter, authorizing them to form and open a lodge of free and accepted masons in the town of ———: They are now desirous that their lodge should be consecrated, and their officers installed in *due and ancient form;* for which purpose they are now met, and await the pleasure of the Most Worshipful Grand Master.

When notice is given, the Grand Lodge walk in procession to the hall of the new Lodge. When the Grand Master enters, the grand honors are given by the new lodge; the officers of which resign their seats to the grand officers, and take their several stations on the left.

The necessary cautions are given; and all, excepting PRESENT or PAST MASTERS of lodges, are requested to retire until, the Master of the new lodge is inducted into the *Oriental Chair of Solomon.* He is then bound to the faithful performance of his trust, and invested with the characteristics of the chair.

Upon due notice, the Grand Marshal re-conducts the brethren into the hall; and all take their places, except the members of the new lodge, who form a procession on one side of the hall. As they advance, the Grand Master addresses them.

"*Brethren, behold your Master.*"

They make the proper salutations as they pass.

A grand procession is then formed, in the following order; viz.

Tyler with a drawn Sword;
Two Stewards with white Rods;
Entered Apprentices;
Fellow-Crafts;
Master Masons;
Stewards;
Junior Deacons;
Senior Deacons;
Secretaries;
Treasurers;
Past Wardens;
Junior Wardens;
Senior Wardens;
Past Masters;
Mark Masters;
Royal Arch Masons;
Select Masters;
Knights Templars;
Masters of Lodges.

Marshal;

The New Lodge.

Tyler with a drawn Sword;
Stewards with white Rods;
Entered Apprentices;
Fellow-Crafts;
Master Masons;
Junior and Senior Deacons;
Secretary and Treasurer;
Two Brethren, carrying the Flooring,* or Lodge;

* Carpet.

Junior and Senior Wardens;
The Holy Writings, carried by the oldest or some suitable member, not in office;
The W. Master;
Music.

The Grand Lodge.

Grand Tyler with drawn Sword;
Grand Stewards with white Rods;
A Brother carrying a Golden Vessel of Corn;*
Two Brethren, carrying the Silver Vessels, one of Wine, the other of Oil;
Grand Secretaries;
Grand Treasurers;
A burning Taper, borne by a Past Master;
A Past Master bearing the Holy Writings, Square and Compasses, supported by two Stewards with white Rods;
Two burning Tapers, borne by two Past Masters;
The Tuscan, and Composite Orders;
The Doric, Ionic, and Corinthian Orders;
Past Grand Wardens;
Marshal;
Past Deputy Grand Masters;
Past Grand Masters;
The Globes;
Clergy and Orator;
R. W. Junior and Senior Grand Wardens;
R. W. Deputy Grand Master;
The Master of the oldest Lodge, carrying the Book of Constitutions;
The M. W. Grand Master;

* Wheat

The Grand Deacons, on a line seven feet apart, on the right and left of the Grand Master, with black rods;
Grand Sword Bearer, with a drawn Sword;
Two Stewards, with white rods.

The Marshals conduct the procession to the church, or house, where the services are to be performed. When the front of the procession arrives at the door, they halt, open to the right and left, and face inward; while the Grand Master and others, in succession, pass through and enter the house.

A platform is erected in front of the pulpit, and provided with seats for the accommodation of the Grand Officers.

The Holy Bible, Square and Compasses, and Book of Constitutions, are placed upon a table in front of the Grand Master: the flooring is then spread in the centre, upon the platform, covered with white satin or linen, and encompassed by the three tapers, and the vessels of *corn, wine,* and *oil.*

SERVICES.

1. A piece of Music.
2. Prayer.
3. An Oration.
4. A piece of Music.
5. The Grand Marshal forms the officers and members of the new Lodge in front of the Grand Master. The Deputy Grand Master addresses the Grand Master as follows:

MOST WORSHIPFUL,

A number of brethren, duly instructed in the mysteries of Masonry, having assembled together at stated periods, by virtue of a dispensation granted them for that purpose, do now desire to be *constituted* into a *regular lodge,* agreeably to the ancient usages and customs of the fraternity.

The dispensation and records are presented to the Grand Master, who examines the records, and, if found correct, proclaims:

The records appear to be correct, and are approved. Upon due deliberation, the Grand Lodge have granted the brethren of this new Lodge a charter, establishing and confirming them in the rights and privileges of a *regular constituted Lodge;* which the Grand Secretary will now read.

After the charter is read, the Grand Master then says,

We shall now proceed, according to ancient usage, to constitute these brethren into a regular Lodge.

Whereupon the several officers of the new Lodge deliver up their jewels and badges to their Master, who presents them, with his own, to the Deputy Grand Master; and he to the Grand Master.

The Deputy Grand Master presents the Master Elect to the Grand Master, saying,

MOST WORSHIPFUL,

I present you Brother ———, whom the members of the Lodge, now to be constituted, have chosen for their Master.

The Grand Master asks them if they remain satisfied with their choice. [*They bow in token of assent.*]

The Master elect then presents, severally, his wardens and other officers, naming them and their respective offices. The Grand Master asks the brethren if they remain satisfied with each and all of them. [*They bow as before.*]

The officers and members of the new Lodge form in front of the Grand Master; and the business of *Consecration* commences with solemn music.

6. *Ceremony of Consecration.*

The Grand Master, attended by the Grand Officers and the Grand Chaplain, form themselves in order round the lodge—all devoutly kneeling.

7. A piece of solemn music is performed while the Lodge is uncovered.

After which, the first clause of the Consecration Prayer is rehearsed, which is follows:

"Great Architect of the universe! Maker and Ruler of all worlds! Deign, from thy celestial temple, from realms of light and glory, to bless us in all the purposes of our present assembly! We humbly invoke thee to give us at this, and at all times, *wisdom* in all our doings, *strength* of mind in all our difficulties, and the *beauty* of harmony in all our communications! Permit us, O thou Author of light and life, great Source of love and happiness, to erect this Lodge, and now solemnly to *consecrate* it to the honor of thy glory!

"Glory be to God on high."

[Response by the brethren.]

"As it was in the beginning, is now, and ever shall be; world without end. Amen."

The Deputy Grand Master takes the Golden Vessel of Corn, and the Senior and Junior Grand Wardens take the Silver Vessels of Wine and Oil, and sprinkle the elements of consecration upon the Lodge.

[The Grand Chaplain then continues:]

"Grant, O Lord our God, that those who are now about to be invested with the government of this Lodge, may be endued with wisdom to instruct their brethren in all their duties. May *brotherly love, relief,* and *truth,* always prevail among the members of this Lodge; and may this bond of union continue to strengthen the Lodges throughout the world!

"Bless all our brethren, wherever dispersed; and grant speedy relief to all who are either oppressed or distressed.

"We affectionately commend to thee, all the members of thy whole family. May they increase in grace, in the knowledge of thee, and in the love of each other.

"Finally: may we finish all our work here below, with thy approbation; and then have our transition from this earthly abode to thy heavenly temple above, there to enjoy light, glory and bliss, ineffable and eternal!

"Glory be to God on high."

[Response by the brethren.]

"As it was in the beginning, is now, and ever shall be. So mote it be. Amen."

8. A piece of solemn music is performed while the Lodge is covered.

9. The Grand Chaplain then dedicates the Lodge in the following terms:

"To the memory of the HOLY ST. JOHNS, we dedicate this Lodge. May every brother revere their character, and imitate their virtues.

"Glory be to God on high."

[Response.]

"As it was in the beginning, is now, and ever shall be, world without end.

"So mote it be. Amen."

10. A piece of music is performed, while the brethren of the new Lodge advance in procession to salute the Grand Lodge, with their hands crossed upon their breasts, and bowing as they pass. They then take their places as they were.

11. The Grand Master then rises, and constitutes the new Lodge in the form following:

"In the name of the Most Worshipful Grand Lodge, I now constitute and form you, my beloved brethren, into a regular Lodge of free and accepted Masons. From henceforth I empower you to meet as a regular lodge, constituted in conformity to the rites of our order, and the charges of our ancient and honorable fraternity;—and may the Supreme Architect of the universe prosper, direct and counsel you, in all your doings.

[Response.]

"So mote it be. Amen."

SECTION SECOND.

Ceremony of Installation.

The Grand Master, or presiding officer, addresses the Master Elect in the words following, viz.

BROTHER,

Previous to your investiture, it is necessary that you should signify your assent to those ancient charges and regulations, which point out the duty of a Master of a Lodge.

I. You agree to be a good man and true, and strictly to obey the moral law.

II. You agree to be a peaceable subject, and cheerfully to conform to the laws of the country in which you reside.

III. You promise not to be concerned in plots and conspiracies against government; but patiently to submit to the decisions of the supreme legislature.

IV. You agree to pay a proper respect to the civil magistrates, to work diligently, live creditably, and act honorably by all men.

V. You agree to hold in veneration, the original rules and patrons of the order of masonry, and their regular successors, supreme and subordinate, according to their stations; and to submit to the awards and resolutions of your brethren, when convened, in every case consistent with the constitutions of the order.

VI. You agree to avoid private piques and quarrels, and to guard against intemperance and excess.

VII. You agree to be cautious in carriage and behavior, courteous to your brethren, and faithful to your lodge.

VIII. You promise to respect genuine brethren, and to discountenance impostors, and all dissenters from the original plan of masonry.

IX. You agree to promote the general good of society, to cultivate the social virtues, and to propagate the knowledge of the art.

X. You promise to pay homage to the Grand Master for the time being, and to his officers when duly installed; and strictly to conform to every edict of the Grand Lodge, or general assembly of masons, that is not subversive of the principles and groundwork of masonry.

XI. You admit that it is not in the power of any men, or body of men, to make innovations in the body of masonry.

XII. You promise a regular attendance on the committees and communications of the Grand Lodge, on receiving proper notice, and to pay attention to all the duties of masonry, on convenient occasions.

XIII. You admit that no new lodge shall be formed without permission of the Grand Lodge: and that no countenance be given to an irregular lodge, or to any person clandestinely initiated therein, being contrary to the ancient charges of the order.

XIV. You admit, that no person can be regularly made a mason in, or admitted a member of, any regular lodge, without previous notice, and due inquiry into his character.

XV. You agree that no visitors shall be received into your lodge, without due examination, and producing proper vouchers of their having been initiated into a regular lodge.

These are the regulations of free and accepted masons.

The presiding officer then addresses the Master as follows:

Do you submit to these charges, and promise to support these regulations, as masters have done in all ages before you?

The Master is to answer, *I do.*

The presiding officer then addresses him:

BROTHER A. B.

In consequence of your cheerful conformity to the charges and regulations of the order, you are now to be installed Master of this * lodge, in full confidence of your care, skill, and capacity to govern the same.

[The new master is then regularly invested with the insignia of his office, and the furniture and implements of his lodge.]

The various implements of the profession are emblematical of our conduct in life, and upon this occasion are carefully enumerated.

The *Holy Writings,* that great light in masonry, will guide you to all truth: it will direct your paths to the temple of happiness, and point out to you the whole duty of man.

---

* If this lodge is installed for the first time, it is called, "*This new Lodge.*"

The *Square* teaches us to regulate our actions by rule and line, and harmonize our conduct by the principles of morality and virtue.

The *Compasses* teach us to limit our desires in every station; that, rising to eminence by merit, we may live respected, and die regretted.

The *Rule* directs that we should punctually observe our duty; press forward in the path of virtue, and, neither inclining to the right nor to the left, in all our actions have (eternity) in view.

The *Line* teaches the criterion of moral rectitude, to avoid dissimulation in conversation and action, and to direct our steps to the path which leads to a glorious immortality.

The *Book of Constitutions,* you are to search at all times. Cause it to be read in your lodge, that none may pretend ignorance of the excellent precepts it enjoins.

You will also receive in charge the *By-Laws* of your lodge, which you are to see carefully and punctually executed.

CHARGE upon the Installation of the Master of a Lodge.

WORSHIPFUL MASTER:

Being appointed Master of this lodge, you cannot be insensible of the obligations which devolve on you, as their head; nor of your responsibility for the faithful discharge of the important duties annexed to your appointment.

The honor, reputation, and usefulness of your lodge, will materially depend on the skill and assiduity with which you manage its concerns; while the happiness of its members will be generally promoted, in proportion to the zeal and ability with which you propagate the genuine principles of our institution.

For a pattern of imitation, consider the great luminary of nature, which, rising in the *East,* regularly diffuses light and luster to all within its circle. In like manner, it is your province to spread and communicate light and instruction to the brethren of your lodge. Forcibly impress upon them the dignity and high importance of masonry, and seriously admonish them never to disgrace it. Charge them to practice out of the lodge, those duties which are taught in it; and by amiable, discreet, and virtuous conduct, to convince mankind of the goodness of the institution; so that, when any one is said to be a member of it, the world may know that he is one to whom the burdened heart may pour out its sorrows; to whom distress may prefer its suit; whose hand is guided by justice, and his heart expanded by benevolence. In short, by a diligent observance of the by-laws of your lodge, the constitutions of masonry, and, above all, the *Holy Scriptures,* which are given as a rule and guide to your faith, you will be enabled to acquit yourself with honor and reputation, and lay up a *crown of rejoicing,* which shall continue when time shall be no more.

The subordinate officers are then severally invested by the presiding officer, who delivers each of them a short Charge, as follows; viz.

The Senior Warden.

BROTHER C. D.

You are appointed Senior Warden of this lodge, and are now invested with the ensign of your office.

The *Level* demonstrates that we are descended from the same stock, partake of the same nature, and share the same hope; and though distinctions among men are necessary to preserve subordination, yet no eminence of station should make us forget that we are brethren: for he who is placed on the lowest spoke of fortune's wheel, may be entitled to our regard; because a time will come, and the wisest knows not how soon, when all distinction, but that of goodness, shall cease; and death, the grand leveler of human greatness, reduce us to the same state.

Your regular attendance on our stated meetings is essentially necessary. In the absence of the master, you are to govern this lodge; in his presence, you are to assist him in the government of it. I firmly rely on your knowledge of masonry, and attachment to the lodge, for the faithful discharge of the duties of this important trust.—*Look well to the West!*

The Junior Warden.

BROTHER E. F.

You are appointed Junior Warden of this lodge and are now invested with the badge of your office.

The *Plumb* admonishes us to walk uprightly in our several stations; to hold the scales of justice in equal poise; to observe the just medium between intemperance and pleasure; and to make our passions and prejudices coincide with the line of our duty.

To you is committed the superintendence of the craft, during the hours of refreshment:—it is therefore indispensably necessary, that you should not only be temperate and discreet, in the indulgence of your own inclinations, but carefully observe that none of the craft be suffered to convert the purposes of refreshment into intemperance and excess.

Your regular and punctual attendance is particularly requested; and I have no doubt that you will faithfully execute the duty which you owe to your present appointment.———*Look well to the South!*

The Treasurer.

BROTHER G. H.

You are appointed Treasurer of this lodge. It is your duty to receive all monies from the hands of the Secretary, make due entries of the same, and pay them out by order of the Worshipful Master and the consent of the lodge.

I trust your regard for the fraternity will prompt you to the faithful discharge of the duties of your office.

The Secretary.

BROTHER J. K.

You are appointed Secretary of this lodge. It is your duty to observe all the proceedings of the lodge; make a fair record of all things proper to be written; to receive all monies due the lodge, and pay them over to the Treasurer, and take his receipt for the same.

Your good inclination to masonry and this lodge, I hope, will induce you to discharge your office with fidelity; and by so doing, you will merit the esteem and applause of your brethren.

Senior and Junior Deacons.

BROTHERS L. M. AND N. O.

You are appointed Deacons of this lodge. To you, with such assistance as may be necessary, is entrusted the examination of visitors.—It is also your province to attend on the master and wardens, and to act as their proxies in the active duties of the lodge; such as in the reception of candidates into the different degrees of masonry, and in the immediate practice of our rites. The Square and Compasses, as badges of your office, I trust to your care, not doubting your vigilance and attention.

The Stewards.

BROTHERS P. Q. AND R. S.

You are appointed Stewards of this lodge. The duties of your office are, to assist in the collection of dues and subscriptions; to keep an account of the lodge expenses; to see that the tables are properly furnished at refreshment, and that every brother is suitably provided for; and generally to assist the deacons and other officers in performing their duties.

Your regular and early attendance will afford the best proof of your zeal and attachment to the lodge.

The Tyler.

BROTHER:

You are appointed Tyler of this lodge; and I invest you with the implement of your office. As the sword is placed in the hands of the Tyler, to enable him effectually to guard against the approach of cowans and eavesdroppers, and suffer none to pass or repass but such as are duly qualified; so it should morally serve as a constant admonition to us, to set a guard at the entrance of our thoughts; to place a watch at the door of our lips; to post a sentinel at the avenue of our actions: thereby excluding every unqualified and unworthy thought, word and deed; and preserving consciences void of offence towards God and towards man.

Your early and punctual attendance will afford the best proof of your zeal for the institution.

CHARGE to the Brethren of the Lodge.

Such is the nature of our constitution that as some must of necessity rule and teach, so others must of course learn to submit and obey. Humility in both is an essential duty. The officers, who are appointed to govern your lodge, are sufficiently conversant with the rules of propriety, and the laws of the institution, to avoid exceeding the powers with which they are entrusted; and you are of too generous dispositions to envy their preferment. I therefore trust that you will have but one aim, to please each other, and unite in the grand design of being happy, and communicating happiness.

Finally, my brethren, as this association has been formed and perfected with so much unanimity and concord, in which we greatly rejoice, so may it long continue. May you long enjoy every satisfaction and delight which disinterested friendship can afford. May kindness and brotherly affection distinguish your conduct, as men, and as masons. Within your peaceful walls, may your children's children celebrate with joy and gratitude, the transactions of this auspicious solemnity. And may *the tenets of our profession* be transmitted through your lodge, pure and unimpaired, from generation to generation.

12. The Grand Marshal then proclaims the new Lodge in the following manner, viz:

In the name of the Most Worshipful Grand Lodge of the State of ———, I proclaim this new Lodge by the name of ——— Lodge, No —, to be legally constituted, consecrated, and the officers thereof duly installed.

13. A piece of Music is then performed.

14. Benediction.

The procession is then formed, and returns in due form to the hall whence it set out.

The W. Master having been previously inducted into the *Oriental Chair of Solomon,* all but master masons are caused to retire.

A procession is then formed, and passes three times round the hall; and upon passing the master, pays him due homage by the usual honors, in the different degrees.

During the procession passing round, the following song is sung.

HAIL MASONRY divine!
Glory of ages shine;
Long may'st thou reign;
Where'er thy lodges stand,
May they have great command
And always grace the land,
Thou Art divine;

Great fabrics still arise,
And grace the azure skies;
Great are thy schemes:
Matchless, beyond compare;
No art with thee can share,
Thou Art divine.

Hiram, the architect,
Did all the craft direct
How they should build:
Sol'mon, great Israel's king,
Did mighty blessings bring,
And left us room to sing,
Hail, royal Art!
} Chorus, three times.

The Grand Master then directs the Grand Marshal to form the procession; when the Grand Lodge walk to their own hall, and both Lodges are closed in due form.

SECTION THIRD.

This section contains the ceremony observed on laying the Foundation Stones of Public Structures.

This ceremony is conducted by the M. W. Grand Master and his officers, assisted by such officers and members of subordinate Lodges, as can conveniently attend. The chief magistrate, and other civil officers of the place where the building is to be erected, also generally attends on the occasion.

At the time appointed, the Grand Lodge is convened in some suitable place. A band of martial music is provided, and the brethren appear in the insignia of the order.

The Lodge is then opened by the Grand Master, and the rules for regulating the procession are read by the Grand Secretary. The Lodge is then adjourned; after which, the procession sets out in *due form,* in the following order:

Procession at laying Foundation Stones.

Two Tylers with drawn Swords;

Tyler of the older Lodge with do.;

Two Stewards of the older Lodge;

Entered Apprentices;

Fellow Crafts;

Master Masons;

Past Secretaries;

Past Treasurers;

Marshal;

Past Junior Wardens;

Past Senior Wardens;

Mark Masters;

Past Masters;

Royal Arch Masons;

Select Masters;

Knights Templars;

Masters;

Music;

Grand Tyler with a drawn Sword;

Grand Stewards with white Rods;

A Past Master with a Golden Vessel containing Corn;

Principal Architect, with Square, Level and Plumb;

Two Past Masters with Silver Vessels, one containing Wine, and the other Oil;

Grand Secretary and Treasurer;

The Five Orders;

One large Light borne by a Past Master;

The Holy Bible, Square and Compasses, borne by a Master of a Lodge, supported by two Stewards on the right and left;

Two large Lights, borne by two Past Masters;

Grand Chaplain;

Clergy and Orator;

Grand Wardens;
Deputy Grand Master;
The Master of the oldest Lodge, carrying the Book of Constitutions on a velvet cushion;
Grand Deacons with black Rods, on a line seven feet apart;
Grand Master;
Two Stewards with white Rods;
Grand Sword-Bearer with drawn Sword.

A Triumphal Arch is usually erected at the place where the ceremony is to be performed. The procession passes through the arch; and the brethren repairing to their stands, the Grand Master and his officers take their places on a temporary platform, covered with carpet. The Grand Master commands silence. An Ode on Masonry is sung; after which, the necessary preparations are made for laying the stone, on which is engraved the year of masonry, the name of the Grand Master, &c. &c.

The stone is raised up, by means of an engine erected for that purpose, and the Grand Chaplain or Orator repeats a short prayer.

The Grand Treasurer then, by the Grand Master's command, places under the stone various sorts of coin and medals of the present age. Solemn music is introduced, and the stone is let down into its place.

The principal Architect then presents the working tools to the Grand Master, who applies the *plumb, square,* and *level,* to the stone, in their proper positions, and pronounces it to be WELL FORMED, TRUE, and TRUSTY.

The Golden and Silver Vessels are next brought to the table, and delivered; the former to the Deputy Grand Master, and the latter to the Grand Wardens, who successively present them to the Grand Master; and he, according to ancient ceremony, pours the corn, the wine, and the oil, which they contain, on the stone; saying,

"May the all-bounteous Author of Nature bless the inhabitants of this place with all the necessaries, conveniences and comforts of life; assist in the erection and completion of this building; protect the workmen against every accident, and long preserve this structure from decay: and grant to us all, a supply of the CORN of *nourishment,* the WINE of *refreshment,* and the OIL of *joy!*

"So mote it be. Amen."

He then strikes the stone thrice with the mallet; and the *public grand honors of Masonry are given.* The Grand Master then delivers over to the Architect the various implements of architecture, entrusting him with the superintendence and direction of the work; after which, he re-ascends the platform, and an Oration suitable to the occasion is delivered.

A voluntary Collection is made for the needy workmen; and the sum collected is placed upon the stone by the Grand Treasurer.

A suitable Song in honor of masonry concludes the ceremony; after which, the procession returns to the place whence it set out, and the Lodge is closed in due form.

SECTION FOURTH.

The fourth section contains the ceremony observed at the Dedication of the Free-Masons' Halls.

On the day appointed, the Grand Master and his officers, accompanied by the members of the Grand Lodge, meet in a convenient room near the place where the ceremony is to be performed, and open in *due and ample form,* in the third degree of masonry.

The Master of the Lodge to which the Hall to be dedicated belongs, being present, addresses the Grand Master, as follows:

MOST WORSHIPFUL,

The brethren of ——— Lodge, being animated with a desire of promoting the honor and interest of the craft, have, at great pains and expense, erected a Masonic Hall, for their convenience and accommodation. They are desirous that the same should be examined by the M. W. GRAND LODGE; and if it should meet their approbation, that it should be solemnly dedicated to Masonic purposes, agreeably to *ancient form.*

The Grand Master then directs the Grand Marshal to form the procession, when they move forward to the Hall to be dedicated. On entering, the music will continue while the procession marches three times round the hall.

The lodge, or flooring, is then placed in the centre; and the Grand Master having taken the chair, under a canopy of state, the Grand Officers, and the Masters and Wardens of the Lodges, repair to the places previously prepared for their reception. The three Lights, and the Gold and Silver Pitchers, with the corn, wine and oil, are placed round the Lodge, at the head of which stands the Altar, with the Holy Bible open, and the Square and Compasses laid thereon, with the Charter, Book of Constitutions, and By-Laws.

An Anthem is sung, and an Exordium on Masonry given; after which, the Architect addresses the Grand Master as follows:

MOST WORSHIPFUL,

Having been entrusted with the superintendence and management of the workmen employed in the construction of this edifice; and having, according to the best of my ability, accomplished the task assigned me; I now return my thanks for the honor of this appointment, and beg leave to surrender up the implements which were committed to my care, when the foundation of this fabric was laid; humbly hoping, that the exertions which have been made on this occasion, will be crowned with your approbation, and that of the Most Worshipful Grand Lodge.

To which the Grand Master makes the following reply:

BROTHER ARCHITECT,

The skill and fidelity displayed in the execution of the trust reposed in you, at the commencement of this undertaking, have secured the entire approbation of the Grand Lodge; and they sincerely pray, that this edifice may continue a lasting monument of the taste, spirit, and liberality of its founders.

An Ode in honor of masonry is sung, accompanied with instrumental music.

The Deputy Grand Master then rises, and says:

MOST WORSHIPFUL,

The hall in which we are now assembled, and the plan upon which it has been constructed, having met with your approbation, it is the desire of the fraternity that it should now be dedicated, according to ancient form and usage.

Whereupon the Grand Master requests all to retire, but such as are Master Masons. A procession is then formed in the following order, viz.

Grand Sword-Bearer;
A Past Master, with a Light;
A Past Master, with Bible, Square, and Compasses, on a velvet cushion;
Two Past Masters, each with a Light;
Grand Secretary and Treasurer, with Emblems;
Grand Junior Warden, with Pitcher of Corn;
Grand Senior Warden, with Pitcher of Wine;
Deputy Grand Master, with Pitcher of Oil;
Grand Master;
Two Stewards with Rods.

All the other brethren keep their places, and assist in performing an Ode, which continues during the procession, excepting only at the intervals of dedication. The Lodge being uncovered, the first time passing round it, the Junior Grand Warden presents the pitcher of Corn to the Grand Master, who pours it out upon the Lodge, at the same time pronouncing,

"In the name of the Great JEHOVAH, to whom be all honor and glory, I do solemnly dedicate this Hall to MASONRY."

The grand honors are given.

The second time passing round the Lodge, the Grand Senior Warden presents the pitcher of Wine to the Grand Master, who sprinkles it upon the Lodge, at the same time saying,

"In the name of the HOLY SAINT JOHNS, I do solemnly DEDICATE this Hall to VIRTUE."

The grand honors are twice given.

The third time passing round the Lodge, the Deputy Grand Master presents the Grand Master with the pitcher of Oil, who sprinkles it upon the Lodge, saying,

"In the name of the whole Fraternity, I do solemnly dedicate this Hall to UNIVERSAL BENEVOLENCE."

The grand honors are thrice given.

A solemn Invocation is made to the Throne of Grace, by the Grand Chaplain, and an Anthem sung; after which, the Lodge is covered, and the Grand Master retires to his Chair.

An Oration is then delivered, and the ceremonies conclude with music.

The Grand Lodge is then closed in due and ample form.

SECTION FIFTH.

This section contains the ceremony observed at Funerals, according to ancient custom; together with the Service used on such occasions.

No mason can be interred with the formalities of the order, unless he has been raised to the sublime degree of Master Mason; as no Fellow Craft or Entered Apprentices are entitled to funeral obsequies, nor to attend the Masonic procession, on such occasions.

All the brethren, who walk in procession, should observe, as much as possible, a uniformity in their dress. Decent mourning around the left arm, with white stockings, gloves and aprons, are most suitable.

The Funeral Service.

The brethren being assembled at the lodge room, (or some other convenient place,) the presiding officer opens the Lodge in the third degree, with the usual forms; and having stated the purpose of the meeting, the service begins:

Master. "What man is he that liveth, and shall not see death? Shall he deliver his soul from the hand of the grave?"

Response. "Man walketh in a vain shadow; he heapeth up riches, and cannot tell who shall gather them."

Master. "When he dieth he shall carry nothing away; his glory shall not descend after him."

Response. "Naked he came into the world, and naked he must return."

Master. "The Lord gave, and the Lord hath taken away: blessed be the name of the Lord!"

The Master then taking the *roll* in his hand, says, "Let us live and die like the righteous, that our last end may be like his!"

The Brethren answer, "God is our God for ever and ever; he will be our guide even unto death!"

The Master then records the name and age of the deceased upon the *roll,* and says,

"Almighty Father! In thy hands we leave with humble submission the soul of our deceased Brother."

The Brethren answer three times, (giving the *grand honors* each time,)

"The will of God is accomplished! So mote it be. Amen."

The Master then deposits the *roll* in the *archives,* and repeats the following Prayer:

"Most glorious God! Author of all good, and giver of all mercy! Pour down thy blessings upon us, and strengthen our solemn engagements with the ties of sincere affection! May the present instance of mortality remind us of our approaching fate, and draw our attention toward thee, the only refuge in time of need! that, when the awful moment shall arrive, that we are about to quit this transitory scene, the enlivening prospect of thy mercy, through the Redeemer, may dispel the gloom of death; and after our departure hence in peace, and in thy favor, may we be received into thine everlasting kingdom, to enjoy, in union with the souls of our departed friends, the just reward of a pious and virtuous life. Amen."

A procession is then formed, which moves to the house of the deceased, and from thence to the place of interment.

Order of Procession at a Funeral.

Tyler with a drawn Sword;
Stewards with white Rods;
Musicians, (if they are masons,) otherwise they follow the Tyler.
Master Masons.
Marshal;
Senior and Junior Deacons;
Secretary and Treasurer;
Senior and Junior Wardens;
Mark Masters;
Past Masters;
Royal Arch Masons;
Select Masters;
Knights Templars;

The Holy Writings, on a cushion, covered with black cloth, carried by the oldest (or some suitable) Member of the Lodge;
The Master;
Clergy;

The Body, with the insignia placed thereon.

Pall Bearers. Pall Bearers.

When the procession arrives at the church yard, the members of the lodge form a circle round the grave; and the clergymen and officers of the lodge take their station at the head of the grave, and the mourners at the foot. The service is resumed, and the following Exhortation is given:

"Here we view a striking instance of the uncertainty of life, and the vanity of all human pursuits. The last offices paid to the dead, are only useful as lectures to the living:—from them we are to derive instruction, and to consider every solemnity of this kind as a summons to prepare for our approaching dissolution.

"Notwithstanding the various mementos of mortality, with which we daily meet; notwithstanding Death has established his empire over all the works of nature; yet, through some unaccountable infatuation, we forget that we are born to die; we go on from one design to another, add hope to hope, and lay out plans for the employment of many years, till we are suddenly alarmed with the approach of Death, when we least expect him, and at an hour which we probably conclude to be the meridian of our existence.

"What are all the externals of majesty, the pride of wealth, or charms of beauty, when Nature has paid her just debt?—Fix your eyes on the last scene, and view life script of her ornaments, and exposed in her natural meanness; you will then be convinced of the futility of those empty delusions. In the grave, all fallacies are detected, all ranks are leveled, and all distinctions are done away.

"While we drop the sympathetic tear over the grave of our deceased friend, let charity incline us to throw a veil over his foibles, whatever they may have been, and not withhold from his memory the praise that his virtues may have claimed. Suffer the apologies of human nature to plead in his behalf. Perfection on earth has never been attained;—the wisest, as well as the best of men, have erred.

"Let the present example excite our most serious thoughts, and strengthen our resolutions of amendment. As life is uncertain, and all earthly pursuits are vain, let us no longer postpone the all-important concern of preparing for eternity; but embrace the happy moment, while time and opportunity offer, to provide against the great change, when all the pleasures of this world shall cease to delight and the reflections of a virtuous and holy life yield the only comfort and consolation. Thus our expectations will not be frustrated, nor we hurried unprepared into the presence of an all-wise and powerful Judge, to whom the secrets of all hearts are known.

"Let us, while in this state of existence, support with propriety the character of our profession, advert to the nature of our solemn ties, and pursue with assiduity the sacred tenets of our order. Then, with becoming reverence, let us seek the favor of the ETERNAL GOD, through the merits of his SON our Savior, so that when the awful moment of Death arrives, be it soon or late, we may be enabled to prosecute our journey without dread or apprehension, to that far distant country, whence no traveler returns."

The following invocations are then made by the Master:

Master. "May we be true and faithful; and may we live and die in love!"

Answer. "So mote it be."

Master. "May we profess what is good, and always act agreeably to our profession!"

Answer. "So mote it be."

Master. "May the Lord bless us and prosper us and may all our good intentions be crowned with success!"

Answer. "So mote it be."

Master. "Glory to be to God in the highest; on earth peace! Good will towards men!"

Answer. "So mote it be, now, from henceforth, and for ever more. Amen."

The apron is taken off from the coffin and handed to the Master—the coffin is deposited in the grave—and the Master says:

This Lamb Skin, or white leather Apron, is an emblem of Innocence, and the badge of a Mason, more ancient than the Golden Fleece or Roman eagle; more honorable than the star and garter, when worthily worn. [*The Master then deposits it in the grave.*] This emblem I now deposit in the grave of our deceased Brother. By this we are reminded of the universal dominion of Death. The arm of Friendship cannot oppose the King of Terrors, nor the charms of innocence elude his grasp. This grave, that coffin, this circle of mourning friends, remind us that we too are mortal: soon shall our bodies molder to dust. Then how important for us that we should know that our REDEEMER liveth, and that he shall stand at the latter day upon the Earth. [*The Master, holding the evergreen in his hand, continues,*] This *evergreen* is an emblem of our faith in the immortality of the soul. By this we are reminded that we have an immortal part within us, which shall survive the grave, and which shall never, never, never die. Though like our Brother whose remains now lie before us, we shall soon be clothed in the habiliments of DEATH and deposited in the silent tomb, yet through the mediation of a divine and ascended Savior, we may confidently hope that our souls will bloom in Eternal Spring.

The brethren then move in procession round the place of interment, and severally drop the sprig of evergreen into the grave; after which, *the public grand honors are given.*

The Master then continues the ceremony at the grave, in the following words:

"From time immemorial, it has been the custom among the fraternity of free and accepted masons, at the request of a brother, to accompany his corpse to the place of interment, and there to deposit his remains with the usual formalities.

"In conformity to this usage, and at the request of our deceased brother, whose memory we revere, and whose loss we now deplore, we have assembled in the character of masons, and to offer up to his memory, before the world, the last tribute of our affection; thereby demonstrating the sincerity of our past esteem, and our steady attachment to the principles of the order.

"The great Creator having been pleased, out of his mercy, to remove our brother from the cares and troubles of a transitory existence, to a state of eternal duration, and thereby to weaken the chain, by which we are united man to man; may we, who survive him anticipate our approaching fate, and be more strongly cemented in the ties of union and friendship; that, during the short space allotted to our present existence, we may wisely and usefully employ our time; and, in the reciprocal of intercourse of kind and friendly acts, mutually promote the welfare and happiness of each other.

"Unto the grave we have resigned the body of our deceased friend, earth to earth, dust to dust, ashes to ashes, there to remain until the trump shall sound on the resurrection morn. We can cheerfully leave him in the hands of a Being who has done all things well; who is glorious in holiness, fearful in praises, doing wonders. Then let us all so improve this solemn warning, that on the great day of account we may receive from the compassionate Judge, the welcome invitation, "Come, ye blessed of my Father, inherit the kingdom prepared for you from the foundation of the world."

"So mote it be. Amen."

"Almighty and eternal God, in whom we live, and move, and have our being—and before whom all men must appear in the judgment day to give an account of their deeds in life; we, who are daily exposed to the lying shafts of death, and now surround the grave of our fallen brother; most earnestly beseech thee to impress deeply on our minds the solemnities of this day, as well as the lamentable occurrence that has occasioned them. Here may we be forcibly reminded, that in the midst of life we are in death, and that whatever *elevation* of character we may have attained; however *upright* and *square* the course we have pursued; yet shortly must we all submit as victims of its destroying power, and endure the humbling *level* of the tomb, until the last loud trump shall sound the summons of our *resurrection* from mortality and *corruption*.

"May we have thy divine assistance, O merciful God, to redeem our mis-spent time; and in the discharge of the important duties thou hast assigned us in the erection of our moral edifice, may we have *wisdom* from on high to direct us, *strength* commensurate with our *task* to support us, and the *beauty* of holiness to adorn and render all our performances acceptable in thy sight: and when our work is done, and our bodies mingle with the *mother earth,* may our souls, disengaged from their cumbrous dust, flourish and bloom in eternal day; and enjoy that rest which thou hast prepared for all good and faithful servants, in that spiritual house, not made with hands, eternal in the heavens, through the great Redeemer. Amen."

"So mote it be. Amen."

The procession then returns in form to the place whence it set out, where the necessary duties are complied with, and the Lodge is closed in the third degree.

NOTE. *If the Grand Master attends, and presides at any ceremony, it is said to be performed in AMPLE FORM;—if a subordinate officer of the Grand Lodge, in DUE FORM;—if vested in the master of a subordinate Lodge, in FORM.*

MOST EXCELLENT MASTER'S DEGREE.

NONE but those who have been inducted into the *Oriental Chair of Solomon,* by the unanimous suffrages of their brethren, can be admitted to this degree of masonry.

When the temple of Jerusalem was finished, and the cap-stone celebrated, with great joy, King Solomon admitted to this degree, only those who had proved themselves worthy, by their virtue, skill, and inflexible fidelity to the craft. The duties incumbent on a Most Excellent Master are such, that he should have a perfect knowledge of all the preceding degrees.

The following Psalm is read at opening.

PSALM 24.

"The earth is the Lord's and the fullness thereof; the world, and they that dwell therein. For he hath founded it upon the seas, and established it upon the floods.—who shall ascend into the hill of the Lord? Or who shall stand in his holy place? He that hath clean hands, and a pure heart; who hath not lifted up his soul unto vanity, nor sworn deceitfully. He shall receive the blessing from the Lord, and righteousness from the God of his salvation. This is the generation of them that seek him, that seek thy face, O Jacob: Selah. Lift up your heads, O ye gates; and be ye lifted up, ye everlasting doors, and the King of Glory shall come in. Who is this King of Glory? The Lord, strong and mighty; the Lord, mighty in battle. Lift up your heads, O ye gates; even lift them up, ye everlasting doors, and the King of Glory shall come in. Who is this King of Glory? The Lord of Hosts, he is the King of Glory. Selah."

The following Psalm is read during the ceremony of receiving a candidate in this degree.

PSALM 122.

"I was glad when they said unto me; Let us go into the house of the Lord. Our feet shall stand within thy gates, O Jerusalem. Jerusalem is builded as a city that is compact together: whither the tribes go up, the tribes of the Lord, unto the testimony of Israel, to give thanks unto the name of the Lord. For there are set thrones of judgment, the thrones of the house of David.

"Pray for the peace of Jerusalem: they shall prosper that love thee. Peace be within thy walls, and prosperity within thy palaces. For my brethren and companions' sakes, I will now say, Peace be within thee. Because of the house of the Lord our God, I will seek thy good."

The following Song is sung with solemn ceremony.

MOST EXCELLENT MASTER'S SONG.

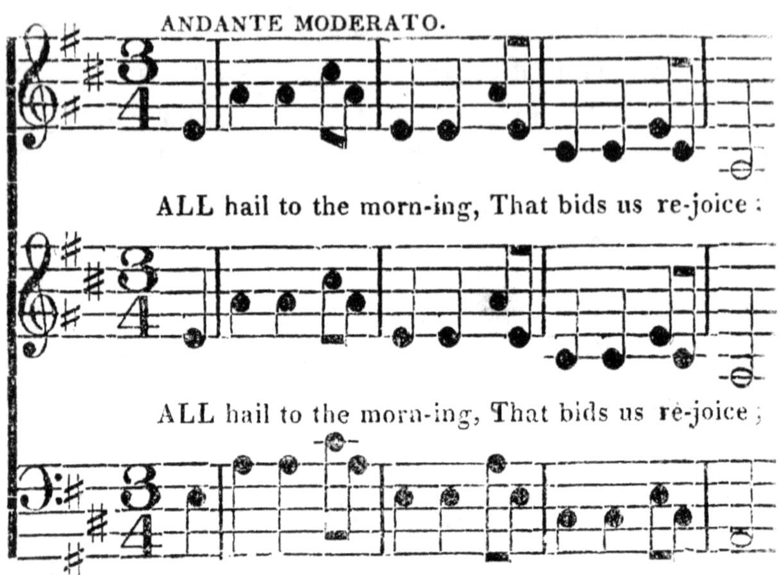

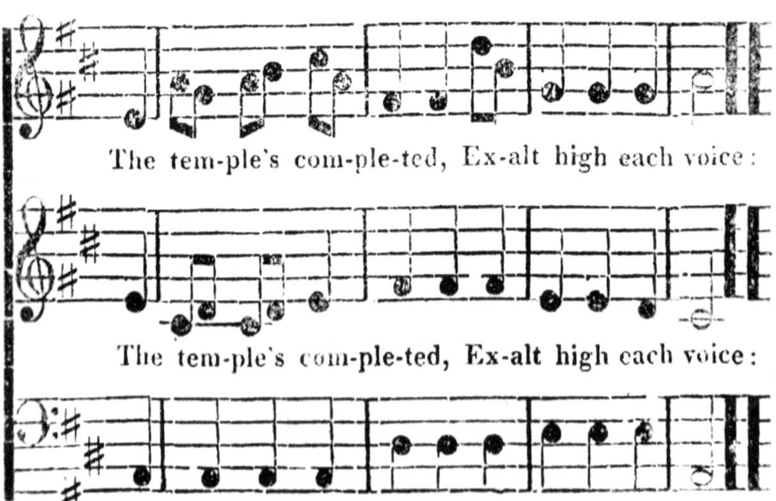

CRES.
The cap-stone is fin-ish'd, Our la - bour is o'er;
The cap-stone is fin-ish'd, Our la - bour is o'er;
The sound of the ga-vel shall hail us no more.
The sound of the ga-vel shall hail us no more.
FOR.
To the Pow-er Al-migh-ty, who ev-er has gui-ded
To the Pow-er Al-migh-ty, who ev-er has gui-ded

The tribes of old Is - rael, ex - alt - ing their fame;
The tribes of old Is - rael, ex - alt - ing their fame;
To Him, who hath go-vern'd our hearts un-di-vi-ded,
To Him, who hath go-vern'd our hearts un-di-vi-ded,
FORTISS.
Let's send forth our voi-ces to praise his great Name.
Let's send forth our voi-ces to praise his great Name.

Companions assemble
On this joyful day;
(The occasion is glorious,)
The key-stone to lay:
Fulfill'd is the promise,
By the ANCIENT OF DAYS,
To bring forth the cap-stone
With shouting and praise.
[*Ceremonies.*]

There is no more occasion for level or plumb-line,
For trowel or gavel, for compass or square:
Our works are completed, the ark safely seated,
And we shall be greeted as workmen most rare.

Now those that are worthy,
Our toils who have shar'd,
And prov'd themselves faithful,
Shall meet their reward.
Their virtue and knowledge,
Industry and skill,
Have our approbation,
Have gain'd our good will.

We accept and receive them, Most Excellent Masters,
Invested with honors, and power to preside;
Among worthy crafts-men, wherever assembled,
The knowledge of masons to spread far and wide.

ALMIGHTY JEHOVAH!
Descend now and fill
This Lodge with thy glory,
Our hearts with good will!
Preside at our meetings,
Assist us to find
True pleasure in teaching
Good will to mankind.

Thy *wisdom* inspired the great institution,
Thy *strength* shall support it till nature expire;
And when the creation shall fall into ruin,
Its *beauty* shall rise through the midst of the fire!

The ceremony closes with the following passage:

2 CHRON. 7:1-4.

Now when Solomon had made an end of praying, the fire came down from heaven, and consumed the burnt offering and sacrifices; and the glory of the Lord filled the house. And the priest could not enter into the house of the Lord, because the glory of the Lord had filled the Lord's house.

And when all the children of Israel saw how the fire came down, and the glory of the Lord upon the house, they bowed themselves with their faces to the ground upon the pavement, and worshipped, and praised the Lord, saying, FOR HE IS GOOD; FOR HIS MERCY ENDURETH FOR EVER.

The following Psalm is read at closing.

PSALM 23.

"The Lord is my shepherd; I shall not want. He maketh me to lie down in green pastures: he leadeth me beside the still waters. He restoreth my soul: he leadeth me in the paths of righteousness for his name's sake. Yea, though I walk through the valley of the shadow of death, I will fear no evil: for thou art with me; thy rod and thy staff they comfort me. Thou preparest a table before me in the presence of mine enemies; thou anointest my head with oil; my cup runneth over. Surely goodness and mercy shall follow me all the days of my life; and I will dwell in the house of the Lord for ever."

CHARGE to a Brother who is received and acknowledged as a most excellent master.

"BROTHER,

"Your admittance to this degree of masonry is a proof of the good opinion the brethren of this lodge entertain of your Masonic abilities. Let this consideration induce you to be careful of forfeiting, by misconduct, and inattention to our rules, that esteem which has raised you to the rank you now possess.

"It is one of your great duties as a most excellent master, to dispense light and truth to the uninformed mason; and I need not remind you of the impossibility of complying with this obligation, without possessing an accurate acquaintance with the lectures of each degree.

"If you are not already completely conversant in all the degrees heretofore conferred on you, remember, that an indulgence, prompted by a belief that you will apply yourself with double diligence to make yourself so, has induced the brethren to accept you.

"Let it therefore be your unremitting study, to acquire such a degree of knowledge and information, as shall enable you to discharge with propriety, the various duties incumbent on you, and to preserve unsullied, the title now conferred upon you, of a MOST EXCELLENT MASTER."

A Description of Solomon's Temple.

This structure, for beauty, magnificence, and expense, exceeded any building which was ever erected. It was built of large stones of white marble, curiously hewn, and so artfully joined together, that they appeared like one entire stone. Its inner *Walls, Beams, Posts, Doors, Floors,* and *Ceilings,* were made of cedar and olive wood, and planks of fir; which were entirely covered with plates of gold, with various beautiful engravings, and adorned with precious jewels of many splendid colors. The nails which fastened those plates were also of gold, with heads of curious workmanship. The roof was of olive wood, covered with gold; and when the sun shone thereon, the reflection from it was of such a *refulgent splendor,* that it dazzled the eyes of all who beheld it. The court in which the temple stood, and the courts without, were adorned on all sides with stately buildings, and cloisters; and the gates entering therein, were exquisitely beautiful and elegant. The vessels consecrated to the perpetual use of the temple, were suited to the magnificence of the edifice in which they were deposited and used.

Josephus states, that there were one hundred and forty thousand of those vessels, which were made of gold, and one million three hundred and forty thousand of silver; ten thousand vestments for the priests, made of silk, with purple girdles; and two millions of purple vestments for the singers. There were also two hundred thousand trumpets, and forty thousand other musical instruments, made use of in the temple, and in worshipping God.

According to the most accurate computation of the number of talents of gold, silver, and brass, lay out upon the temple, the sum amounts to six thousand nine hundred and four millions, eight hundred and twenty-two thousand and five hundred pounds sterling; and the jewels are reckoned to exceed this sum. The gold vessels are estimated at five hundred and forty-five millions, two hundred and ninety-six thousand, two hundred and three pounds, and four shillings, sterling; and the silver ones, at four hundred and thirty-nine millions, three hundred and forty-four thousand pounds sterling; amount in all, to nine hundred and eighty-four millions, six hundred and thirty thousand, two hundred and thirty pounds, four shillings. In addition to this, there were expenses for workmen, and for materials brought from Mount Libanus, and the quarries of Zeradatha. There were ten thousand men per month in Lebanon, employed in falling and preparing the timbers for the craftsmen to hew them; seventy thousand to carry burdens; eighty thousand to hew the stones and timber; and three thousand three hundred overseers of the work; who were all employed for seven years; to whom, besides their wages and diet, King Solomon gave, as a free gift, six millions, seven hundred and thirty-three thousand, nine hundred and seventy-seven pounds.

The treasure left by David, towards carrying on this noble and glorious work, is reckoned to be nine hundred and eleven millions, four hundred and sixteen thousand, two hundred and seven pounds; to which, if we add King Solomon's annual revenue, his trading to Ophir for gold, and the presents made him by all the earth, as mentioned 1 Kings 10:24-25, we shall not wonder at his being able to carry on so expensive a work; nor can we, without impiety, question its surpassing all other structures, since we are assured that it was built by the immediate direction of HEAVEN.

ROYAL ARCH DEGREE.

THIS degree is more august, sublime, and important, than all which precede it. It impresses on our minds a belief of the being and existence of the Supreme Grand High Priest of our Salvation; who is without beginning of days or end of years; and forcibly reminds us of the reverence due to his Holy Name.

In this degree is brought to light many essentials which are of importance to the craft that were concealed in darkness for the space of four hundred and seventy years; and without a knowledge of which the Masonic character cannot be complete.

SECTION FIRST.

This section explains the mode of government in this degree; it designates the appellation, number and situation of the several officers, and points out the purpose and duty of their respective stations. The various colors of their banners are designated; and the morals to which they allude are introduced and explained.

The following passage of scripture is read at opening:

2 THESS. 3:6-18.

Now we command you, brethren, in the name of our Lord Jesus Christ that ye withdraw yourselves from every brother that walketh disorderly, and not after the tradition which ye received of us. For yourselves know how ye ought to follow us: for we behaved not ourselves disorderly among you; neither did we eat any man's bread for naught; but wrought with labor and travel night and day, that we might not be chargeable to any of you; not because we have not power, but to make ourselves an ensample unto you to follow us. For even when we were with you, this we commanded you, that if any would not work, neither should he eat. For we hear that there are some which walk among you disorderly, working not at all, but are busybodies. Now them that are such we command and exhort, by our Lord Jesus Christ, that with quietness they work, and eat their own bread. But ye, brethren, be not weary in well doing. And if any man obeys not our word by this epistle, note that man, and have no company with him, that he may be ashamed. Yet count him not as an enemy, but admonish him as a brother. Now the Lord of peace himself gives you peace always by all means. The Lord be with you all.

The salutation of Paul with mine own hand, which is the token in every epistle: so I write. The grace of our Lord Jesus Christ be with you all. Amen.

SECTION SECOND.

This section contains much valuable historical information, and exhibits to our view, in striking colors, that prosperity and happiness are ever the ultimate consequences of virtue and justice; while disgrace and ruin invariably follow the practices of vice and immorality.

The following charges and passages of scripture are introduced during the ceremony of Exaltation

ISAIAH 43:16.

"I will bring the blind by a way that they knew not; I will lead them in paths that they have not known; I will make darkness light before them, and crooked things straight. These things will I do unto them, and will not forsake them."

Prayer used at the Exaltation of a Royal Arch Mason.

O thou eternal and omnipotent JEHOVAH, the glorious and everlasting I AM, permit us, thy frail, dependent and needy creatures, in the name of our *Most Excellent and Supreme High Priest,* to approach thy divine majesty. And do thou, who sittest *between the Cherubim,* incline thine ear to the voice of our praises, and of our supplication; and vouchsafe to commune with us from off the *mercy seat.* We humbly adore and worship thy unspeakable perfections, and thy unbounded goodness and benevolence. We bless thee that when man had sinned, and fallen from his innocence and happiness, thou didst still leave unto him the powers of reasoning, and the capacity of improvement and of pleasure. We adore thee, that amidst the pains and calamities of our present state, so many means of refreshment and satisfaction are afforded us, while traveling the *rugged path of life.* And O, thou who didst aforetime appear unto thy servant Moses *in a flame of fire, out of the midst of a bush,* enkindle, we beseech thee, in each of our hearts, a flame of devotion to thee, of love to each other and of benevolence and charity to all mankind. May the *veils* of ignorance and blindness be removed from the eyes of our understandings, that we may behold and adore thy mighty and wondrous works. May the *rod* and staff of thy grace and power continually support us, and defend us from the rage of all our enemies, and especially from the subtlety and malice of that old *serpent,* who with cruel vigilance seeketh our ruin. May the *leprosy* of sin be eradicated from our *bosoms;* and may *Holiness to the Lord* be engraved upon all our thoughts, words and actions. May the *incense* of piety ascend continually unto thee, from off the *altar* of our hearts, and *burn day and night,* as a sweet-smelling savor unto thee. May we daily *search* the records of *truth,* that we may be more and more instructed in our duty; and may we share the blessedness of those who hear the *sacred word, and keep it.* And finally, O merciful Father, when we shall have passed through the outward *veils* of these earthly *courts,* when the earthly house of this *tabernacle* shall be dissolved, may we be admitted into the *Holy of Holies* above, into the presence of the *Grand Council* of heaven, where the Supreme *High Priest* for ever presides, for ever reigns. Amen. *So mote it be.*

EXODUS 3:1-6.

"Now Moses kept the flock of Jethro his father-in-law, the priest of Midian; and he led the flock to the back side of the desert, and came to the mountain of God, even to Horeb. And the angel of the Lord appeared unto him in a flame of fire, out of the midst of a bush; and he looked, and behold the bush burned with fire, and the bush was not consumed.

"And when the Lord saw that he turned aside to see, God called to him out of the bush, and said, Moses, Moses! And he said. Here am I. And he said, Draw not nigh hither: put off thy shoes from off thy feet, for the place whereon thou standest is holy ground. Moreover he said, I am the God of thy father, the God of Abraham, the God of Isaac, and the God of Jacob. And Moses hid his face: for he was afraid to look upon God."

2 CHRON. 36:11-20.

Zedekiah was one and twenty years old, when he began to reign, and he reigned eleven years in Jerusalem. And he did that which was evil in the sight of the Lord his God, and humbled not himself before Jeremiah the prophet, speaking from the mouth of the Lord. And he also rebelled against king Nebuchadnezzar, and stiffened his neck, and hardened his heart, from turning unto the Lord God of Israel. Moreover all the chief of the priests and the people transgressed very much, after all the abominations of the heathen and polluted the house of the Lord, which he had hallowed in Jerusalem. And the Lord God of their fathers sent to them by his messengers, because he had compassion on his people, and on his dwelling place. But they mocked the messengers of God, and despised his word, and misused his prophets, until the wrath of the Lord arose against his people, till there was no remedy.

Therefore he brought upon them the king of the Chaldees, who slew their young men with the sword, in the house of their sanctuary, and had no compassion upon young men or maidens, old men, or him that stooped for age; he gave them all into his hand. And all the vessels of the house of God, great and small, and the treasures of the house of the Lord, and the treasures of the King, and his princes: all these he brought to Babylon.

And they burnt the house of God, and brake down the wall of Jerusalem, and burnt all the palaces thereof with fire, and destroyed all the goodly vessels thereof. And them that had escaped from the sword, carried he away to Babylon;—where they were servants to him and his sons, until the reign of the kingdom of Persia.

EZRA 1:1-3.

Now, in the first year of Cyrus, King of Persia, the Lord stirred up the spirit of Cyrus, King of Persia, that he made a proclamation throughout all his kingdom, and put it also in writing, saying, Thus saith Cyrus, King of Persia, The Lord God of Heaven hath given me all the kingdoms of the earth, and he hath charged me to build him an house at Jerusalem, which is in Judah.—Who is there among you of all his people? His God be with him, and let him go up to Jerusalem, which is in Judah, and build the house of the Lord God of Israel, which is in Jerusalem.

EXODUS 3:13-14.

And Moses said unto God, Behold, when I come unto the children of Israel, and shall say unto them, The God of your fathers hath sent me unto you; and they shall say to me, What is his name? what shall I say unto them?

And God said unto Moses, I AM THAT I AM: And thus thou shalt say unto the children of Israel; I AM hath sent me unto you.

PSALM 141.

Lord, I cry unto thee: make haste unto me; give ear unto my voice. Let my prayer be set forth before thee as incense, and the lifting up of hands as the evening sacrifice. Set a watch, O Lord, before my mouth; keep the door of my lips. Incline not my heart to any evil thing, to practice wicked works with men that work iniquity. Let the righteous smite me, it shall be a kindness; let him reprove me, it shall be an excellent oil. Mine eyes are unto thee, O God the Lord; in thee is my trust; leave not my soul destitute. Keep me from the snares which they have laid for me, and the gins of the workers of iniquity. Let the wicked fall into their own nets, while that I withal escape.

PSALM 142.

I cried unto the Lord with my voice; with my voice unto the Lord did I make my supplication. I poured out my complaint before him: I shewed before him my trouble. When my spirit was overwhelmed within me, then thou knewest my path: in the way wherein I walked, have they privily laid a snare for me. I looked on my right hand, and beheld, but there was no man that would know me: refuge failed me: no man cared for my soul. I cried unto thee, O Lord: I said, Thou art my refuge, and my portion in the land of the living. Attend unto my cry; for I am brought very low:

deliver me from my persecutors; for they are stronger than I. Bring my soul out of darkness, that I may praise thy name.

PSALM 143.

Hear my prayer, O Lord; give ear to my supplication. In thy faithfulness answer me, and in thy righteousness. And enter not into judgment with thy servant: for in thy sight shall no man living be justified. For the enemy hath persecuted my soul; he hath made me to dwell in darkness. Therefore is my spirit overwhelmed within me; my heart within me is desolate. Hear me speedily, O Lord; my spirit faileth; hide not thy face from me, lest I be like them that go down into the pit. Cause me to hear thy loving kindness in the morning; for in thee do I trust: cause me to know the way wherein I should walk; for I lift up my soul unto thee. Teach me to do thy will; for thou art my God: bring my soul out of trouble, and of thy mercy cut off mine enemies, for I am thy servant.

EXODUS 4:1-10.

"And Moses answered and said, But behold, they will not believe me, nor hearken unto my voice: for they will say, The Lord hath not appeared unto thee. And the Lord said unto him, What is that in thine hand? And he said, A rod. And he said, Cast it on the ground: and he cast it on the ground, and it became a serpent; and Moses fled from before it. And the Lord said unto Moses, Put forth thine hand, and take it by the tail. And he put forth his hand and caught it, and it became a rod in his hand. That they may believe that the Lord God of your fathers, the God of

Abraham, the God of Isaac, and the God of Jacob, hath appeared unto thee.

"And the Lord said furthermore unto him, Put now thine hand into thy bosom; and he put his hand into his bosom; and when he took it out, behold, his hand was leprous as snow. And he said, Put thine hand into thy bosom again; and he put his hand into his bosom again; and he plucked it out of his bosom, and, behold, it was turned again as his other flesh. And it shall come to pass, if they will not believe thee, neither hearken to the voice of the first sign, that they will believe the voice of the latter sign.

"And it shall come to pass, if they will not believe also these two signs, neither hearken unto thy voice, that thou shalt take of the water of the river, and pour it upon the dry land: and the water which thou takest out of the river, shall become blood upon the dry land."

HAGGAI 2:2-4, 23.

Speak now to Zerubbabel, the son of Shealtiel, governor of Judah, and to Joshua, the son of Josedec, the high priest, and to the residue of the people, saying, who is left among you, that saw this house in her first glory? And how do you see it now? Is it not, in your eyes, in comparison of it, as nothing? Yet now be strong, O Zerubbabel; and be strong, O Joshua, son of Josedec the high priest; and be strong, all ye people of the land, saith the Lord, and work: for I am with you, saith the Lord of hosts.

"In that day, will I take thee, O Zerubbabel, my servant, the son of Shealtiel, saith the Lord, and will make thee as a signet: for I have chosen thee."

ZECHARIAH 4:9-10.

The hands of Zerubbabel have laid the foundation of this house; his hands shall also finish it; *and thou shalt know that the Lord of hosts hath sent me unto you.* For who hath despised the day of small things? for they shall rejoice, and shall see the plummet in the hand of Zerubbabel, with those seven.

AMOS 9:11.

"In that day will I raise up the tabernacle of David that is fallen, and close up the breaches thereof, and I will raise up his ruins, and I will build it as in the days of old."

The following passages of scripture are read by the High Priest.

GENESIS 1:1-3.

In the beginning God created the heaven and the earth. And the earth was without form and void; and darkness was upon the face of the deep; and the Spirit of God moved upon the face of the waters.—And God said, Let there be light: and there was light.——DEUT. 31:24-26. And it came to pass when Moses had made an end of writing the words of this law in a book, until they were finished, that Moses commanded the Levites which bare the ark of the covenant of the Lord, saying, Take this book of the law, and put it in the side of the ark of the covenant of the Lord your God, that it may be there for a witness against thee.——EXODUS 20:21. And thou shalt put the mercy seat above, upon the ark; and in the ark thou shalt put the testimony that I shall give thee.——EXODUS 16:32-34. And Moses said, This is the thing which the Lord commandeth, Fill an omer of the manna, to be kept for your generations; that they may see the bread wherewith I have fed you in the wilderness, when I brought you forth from the land of Egypt. And Moses said unto Aaron, Take a pot, and put an omer full of manna therein, and lay it up before the Lord, to be kept for your generations. As the Lord commanded Moses, so Aaron laid it up before the testimony to be kept.——NUMBERS 17:10. And the Lord said unto Moses, Bring Aaron's rod again before the testimony, to be kept for a token.——HEBREWS 9:2-5. For there was a tabernacle made; the first, wherein was the candlestick, and the table, and the shew-bread, which is called the Sanctuary. And after the veils, the tabernacle, which is called the Holiest of all; which had the golden censer, and the ark of the covenant, overlaid round about with gold, wherein was the golden pot that had manna, and Aaron's rod that budded, and the tables of the covenant; and over it, the cherubims of glory, shadowing the mercy seat; of which we cannot now speak particularly.

EXODUS 6:2-3.

"And God spoke unto Moses, and said unto him, I am the Lord: and I appeared unto Abraham, unto Isaac, and unto Jacob, by the name of God Almighty; but by my name JEHOVAH was I not known to them."

The High Priest will then recite the following passage, previous to investing the candidate with an important secret of the degree.

JOHN 1:1-5.

"In the beginning was the Word: and the Word was with God, and the word was God. The same was in the beginning with God. All things were made by him: and without him was not any thing made that was made. In him was life, and the life was the light of men. And the light shineth in darkness, and the darkness comprehendeth it not."

The following remarks relative to King Solomon's Temple, cannot be uninteresting to a Royal Arch Mason.

This famous fabric was situated on Mount Moriah, near the place where Abraham was about to offer up his son Isaac, and where David met and appeased the destroying angel, who was visible over the *threshing floor of Ornan the Jebusite.* It was begun in the fourth year of the reign of Solomon; the third after the death of David; four hundred and eighty years after the passage of the Red Sea, and on the second day of the month Zif, being the second month of the sacred year, which answers to the 21st of April, in the year of the world two thousand nine hundred and ninety-two; and was carried on with such prodigious speed, that it was finished, in all its parts, in little more than seven years.

By the Masonic art, and the wise regulations of Solomon, this famous edifice was erected without the sound of the axe, hammer, or any tool of iron; for the stones were all hewed, squared and numbered, in the quarries of Zeradathah, where they were raised; the timbers were fitted and prepared in the forest of Lebanon, and conveyed by sea in floats to Joppa, and from thence by land to Jerusalem; where the fabric was erected by the assistance of wooden instruments prepared for that purpose. And when the building was finished, its several parts fitted with that exact nicety, that it had more the appearance of being the handy work of the Supreme Architect of the Universe, than of human hands.

In the year of the world 3029, King Solomon died, and was succeeded by his son Rehoboam. Soon after this, instigated and led on by Jeroboam, the son of Nebat, ten of the tribes revolted from Rehoboam, and set up a separate kingdom, with Jeroboam at their head. In this manner were the tribes of Israel divided, and under two distinct governments, for two hundred and fifty-four years. The ten revolted tribes became weak and degenerated; their country was laid waste, and their government overthrown and extirpated by Salmanezer, King of Assyria. After a series of changes and events, Nebuchadnezzar, King of Babylon, having besieged Jerusalem, and raised towers all round the city, so that, after defending it for the space of a year and a half, it was, in the eleventh year of the reign of Zedekiah, King of Judah, surrendered and delivered at midnight to the officers of Nebuchadnezzar, who sacked and destroyed the temple, and took away all the holy vessels, together with those two famous brazen pillars; and the remnant of the people that escaped the sword, carried he away captives to Babylon, where they remained servants to him and his successors, until the reign of Cyrus, King of Persia. Cyrus, in the first year of his reign, being directed by that divine power which invisibly led him to the throne of Persia, issued his famous edict for the liberation of the Hebrew captives, with permission that they should return to their native country, and rebuild the city and *house of the Lord.* Accordingly, the principal people of the tribes of Judah and Benjamin, with the Priests and Levites, immediately departed for Jerusalem, and commenced the great and glorious work.

CHARGE to a newly Exalted Companion.

WORTHY COMPANION,

By the consent and assistance of the members of this Chapter, you are now exalted to the sublime and honorable degree of Royal Arch Mason. The rites and mysteries developed in this degree, have been handed down through a chosen few, unchanged by time and uncontrolled by prejudice; and we expect and trust, they will be regarded by you with the same veneration, and transmitted with the same scrupulous purity, to your successors.

No one can reflect on the ceremonies of gaining admission into this place, without being forcibly struck with the important lessons which they teach. Here we are necessarily led to contemplate, with gratitude and admiration, the sacred Source from whence all earthly comforts flow.—Here we find additional inducements to continue steadfast and immoveable in the discharge of our respective duties; and here we are bound by the most solemn ties, to promote each other's welfare, and correct each other's failings, by advice, admonition, and reproof. As it is our earnest desire, and a duty we owe to our companions of this order, that the admission of every candidate into this chapter, should be attended by the approbation of the most scrutinizing eye, we hope always to possess the satisfaction of finding none among us, but such as will promote, to the utmost of their power, the great end of our institution. By paying due attention to this determination, we expect you will never recommend any candidate to this Chapter, whose abilities, and knowledge of the preceding degrees, you cannot freely vouch for, and whom you do not firmly and confidently believe, will fully conform to the principles of our order, and fulfill the obligations of a Royal Arch Mason. While such are our members, we may expect to be united in one object, without Luke warmness, inattention or neglect; but zeal, fidelity and affection, will be the distinguishing characteristics of our society; and that satisfaction, harmony and peace, may be enjoyed at our meetings, which no other society can afford.

Closing Prayer.

By the *wisdom* of the Supreme High Priest, may we be directed; by his *strength,* may we be enabled; and by the *beauty* of virtue, may we be incited, to perform the obligations here enjoined on us; to keep inviolably the mysteries here unfolded to us; and invariably to practice all those duties out of the Chapter, which are inculcated in it.

[Response.] So mote it be. Amen.

ROYAL MASTER'S DEGREE.

THIS degree cannot legally be conferred on any but Royal Arch Masons, who have taken all the preceding degrees; and it is preparatory to that of the Select Master. Although it is short, yet it contains some valuable information, and is intimately connected with the degree of Select Master. It also enables us with ease and facility to examine the privileges of others to this degree; while, at the same time, it proves ourselves.

The following passages of scripture, &c. are considered to be appropriate to this degree.

1 KINGS 7:48-50, and 40.

And Solomon made all the vessels that pertained unto the house of the Lord: the altar of gold, and the table of gold, whereupon the shew-bread was; and the candlesticks of pure gold; five on the right side, and five on the left, before the oracle; with the flowers, and the lamps, and the tongs of gold; and the bowls, and the snuffers, and the basins, and the spoons, and the censers, of pure gold; and the hinges of gold, both for the doors of the inner house, the most holy place, and for the doors of the house, to wit, of the Temple. So Hiram made an end of doing all the work, that he had made King Solomon, for the house of the Lord.

REV. 22:12-14.

And behold I come quickly; and my reward is with me, to give every man according as his work shall be. I am Alpha and Omega, the beginning and the end, the first and the last. Blessed are they that do his commandments that they may have a right to the tree of life, and may enter in through the gates into the city.

1 KINGS 6:27.

And he set the cherubims within the inner house; and they stretched forth the wings of the cherubims, so that the wing of the one touched the one wall; and the wing of the other cherub touched the other wall; and their wings touched one another in the midst of the house.

The Ark, called the glory of Israel, which was seated in the middle of the holy place, under the wings of the cherubim, was a small chest, or coffer, three feet nine inches long, two feet three inches wide, and three feet three inches high. It was made of wood, excepting only the mercy seat, but overlaid with gold, both inside and out. It had a ledge of gold surrounding it at the top, into which the cover, called the mercy seat, was let in. The mercy seat was of solid gold, the thickness of a hand's breadth: at the two ends of it were two cherubims, looking inwards towards each other, with their wings expanded; which embracing the whole circumference of the mercy seat, they met on each side, in the middle; all of which, the Rabbins say, was made out of the same mass, without any soldering of parts.

Here the Shekinah, or Divine Presence, rested, and was visible in the appearance of a cloud over it. From hence the Bathkoll issued, and gave answers when God was consulted. And hence it is that God is said, in the scripture, to dwell between the cherubim; that is, between the cherubim on the mercy seat, because there was the seat or throne of the visible appearance of his glory among them.

SELECT MASTER'S DEGREE.

THIS degree is the summit and perfection of ancient masonry; and without which the history of the Royal Arch Degree cannot be complete. It rationally accounts for the concealment and preservation of those essentials of the craft, which were brought to light at the erection of the second Temple, and which lay concealed from the Masonic eye four hundred and seventy years.

Many particulars relative to those few who, for their superior skill, were selected to complete an important part of King Solomon's Temple, are explained.

And here too is exemplified an instance of *justice* and *mercy,* by our ancient patron, towards one of the craft, who was led to disobey his commands, by an over *zealous* attachment for the institution. It ends with a description of a particular circumstance, which characterizes the degree.

The following Psalm is read at opening:

PSALM 87.

"His foundation is in the holy mountains. The Lord loveth the gates of Zion more than all the dwellings of Jacob. Glorious things are spoken of thee, O city of God. Selah. I will make mention of Rahab and Babylon, to them that know me. Behold Philistia, and Tyre, with Ethiopia; this man was born there. And of Zion it shall be said, This and that man was born in her; and the highest himself shall establish her. The Lord shall count, when he writeth up the people, that this man was born there. Selah. As well the singers, as the players on instruments, shall be there: all my springs are in thee."

The following passages of scripture are introduced and explained:

1 KINGS 4:1, 5 and 6.

So King Solomon was king over all Israel. Azariah, the son of Nathan, was over the officers; and Zabud, the son of Nathan, was principal officer, and the king's friend; and Ahishar was over the household; and Adoniram, the son of Abda, was over the tribute.

1 KINGS 5:17-18.

And the king commanded, and they brought great stones, costly stones, and hewed stones, to lay the foundation of the house. And Solomon's builders and Hiram's builders did hew them, and the stone-squarers: so they prepared timber and stones to build the house.

1 KINGS 8:13-14.

And King Solomon sent and fetched Hiram out of Tyre. He was a widow's son, of the tribe of Naphtali; and his father was a man of Tyre, a worker of brass; and he was filled with wisdom and understanding, and cunning, to work all works in brass.

EZEKIEL 27:9.

The ancients of Gebal, and the wise men thereof, were in thee thy calkers: all the ships of the sea, with their mariners, were in thee, to occupy thy merchandize.

DEUT. 31:24-26.

And it came to pass, when Moses had made an end of writing the words of this law in a book, until they were finished, that Moses commanded the Levites, which bore the ark of the covenant of the Lord, saying, Take this book of the law, and put it in the side of the ark of the covenant of the Lord your God, that it may be there for a witness against thee.

EXODUS 16:33-34.

And Moses said unto Aaron, Take a pot, and put an omer full of manna therein, and lay it up before the Lord, to be kept for your generations. As the Lord commanded Moses, so Aaron laid it up before the testimony to be kept.

NUMBERS 17:10.

And the Lord said unto Moses, Bring Aaron's rod again before the testimony, to be kept for a token.

NUMBERS 7:89.

And when Moses was gone into the tabernacle of the congregation, to speak with him, then he heard the voice of one speaking unto him from off the mercy seat, that was upon the ark of the testimony, from between the two cherubims: and he spake unto him.

EXODUS 25:40.

And look that thou make them after their pattern, which was shewed thee in the mount.

CHARGE to a Select Master.

COMPANION,

Having attained to this degree, you have passed the *circle of perfection* in ancient masonry. In the capacity of Select Master, you must be sensible that your obligations are increased in proportion to your privileges. Let it be your constant care to prove yourself worthy of the confidence reposed in you, and of the high honor conferred on you, in admitting you to this select degree. Let uprightness and integrity attend your steps; let *justice* and *mercy* mark your conduct; let *fervency* and *zeal* stimulate you in the discharge of the various duties incumbent on you; but suffer not an idle or impertinent *curiosity* to lead you astray, or betray you into danger. Be *deaf* to every insinuation which would have a tendency to weaken your resolution, or tempt you to an act of *disobedience.* Be voluntarily *dumb* and *blind,* when the exercise of those faculties would endanger the peace of your mind or the probity of your conduct; and let *silence* and *secrecy,* those cardinal virtues of a Select Master, on all necessary occasions, be scrupulously observed. By a steady adherence to the important instructions contained in this degree, you will merit the approbation of the select number with whom you are associated, and will enjoy the high satisfaction of having acted well your part in the important enterprise in which you are engaged; and after having *wrought your regular hours,* may you be admitted to participate in all the privileges of a *Select Master.*

ORDER OF HIGH PRIESTHOOD.

THIS order appertains to the office of High Priest of a Royal Arch Chapter: and no one can be legally entitled to receive it, until he has been duly elected to preside as High Priest in a regular Chapter of Royal Arch Masons. This order should not be conferred when a less number than three duly qualified High Priests are present. Whenever the ceremony is performed in due and ample form, the assistance of at least nine High Priests, who have received it, is requisite.

Though the High Priest of every regular Royal Arch Chapter, having himself been duly qualified, can confer the order, under the preceding limitation as to number; yet it is desirable, when circumstances will permit, that it should be conferred by the Grand High Priest of the Grand Royal Arch Chapter, or such Present or Past High Priest as he may designate for that purpose. A convention, notified to meet at the time of any convocation of the Grand Chapter, will afford the best opportunity of conferring this important and exalted degree of masonry, with appropriate solemnity. Whenever it is conferred, the following directions are to be observed.

A candidate desirous of receiving the order of High Priesthood makes a written request to his predecessor in office, or, when it can be done, to the Grand High Priest, respectfully requesting that a convention of High Priests may be called, for the purpose of conferring on him the order. When the convention meets, and is duly organized, a certificate of the due election of the candidate to the office of High Priest, must be produced. This certificate is signed by his predecessor in office, attested by the Secretary of the Chapter. On examination of this certificate, the qualifications of the candidate are ascertained. The solemn ceremonies of conferring the order upon him then ensue. When ended, the presiding officer directs the Secretary of the convention to make a record of the proceedings, and return it to the Secretary of the Grand Chapter, to be by him laid before the Grand High Priest, for the information of all whom it may concern. The convention of High Priests is then dissolved in due form.

It is the duty of every Companion, as soon after his election to the office of High Priest, as is consistent with his personal convenience, to apply for admission to the order of High Priesthood, that he may be fully qualified properly to govern his Chapter.

The following passages of scripture are made use of during the ceremonies appertaining to this order.

GENESIS 14:12-24.

And they took Lot, Abram's brother's son, (who dwelt in Sodom,) and his goods, and departed. And there came one that had escaped, and told Abram, the Hebrew; for he dwelt in the plain of Mamre the Amorite, brother of Eshcol, and brother of Aner; and these were confederate with Abram. And when Abram heard that his brother was taken captive, he armed his trained servants, born in his own house, three hundred and eighteen, and pursued them unto Dan. And he divided himself against them, he and his servants, by night, and smote them, and pursued them unto Hobah, which is on the left hand of Damascus. And he brought back all the goods, and also brought again his brother Lot, and his goods, and the women also, and the people.

And the king of Sodom went out to meet him, (after his return from the slaughter of Chedorlaomer, and of the kings that were with him,) at the valley of Shevah, which is the king's dale. And Melchisedek, king of Salem, brought forth bread and wine: and he was the priest of the Most High God. And he blessed him, and said, Blessed be Abram of the Most High God, who hath delivered thine enemies into thy hand. And he gave him tithes of all. And the king of Sodom said to Abram, Give me the persons, and take the goods to thyself. And Abram said to the king of Sodom, I have lifted up mine hand to the Lord, the Most High God, the possessor of heaven and earth, that I will not take from a thread even to a shoe-latchet; and that I will not take any thing that is thine, lest thou shouldest say, I have made Abram rich: save only that which the young men have eaten, and the portion of the men which went with me, Aner, Eshcol and Mamre, let them take their portion.

NUMBERS 6:22-26.

And the Lord spoke unto Moses, saying, Speak unto Aaron, and unto his sons, saying, On this wise ye shall bless the children of Israel, saying unto them, The Lord bless thee, and keep thee; the Lord make his face to shine upon thee, and be gracious unto thee; the Lord lift up his countenance upon thee, and give thee peace.

HEB. 7:1-6.

For this Melchisedek, king of Salem, priest of the Most High God, (who met Abram returning from the slaughter of the kings, and blessed him; to whom also Abraham gave a tenth part of all; first being, by interpretation, King of Righteousness, and after that also, King of Salem, which is, King of Peace; without father, without mother, without descent; having neither beginning of days, nor end of life; but made like unto the Son of God,) abideth a priest continually. Now consider how great this man was, unto whom even the patriarch Abraham gave the tenth of the spoils. And verily, they that are of the sons of Levi, who receive the office of the priesthood, have a commandment to take tithes of the people, according to the law, that is, of their brethren, though they come out of the loins of Abraham.

"For he testifieth, Thou art a priest for ever, after the order of Melchisedek.

"And inasmuch as not without an oath, he was made priest.

"For those priests (under the Levitical law) were made without an oath; but this with an oath, by him that said unto him, The Lord sware, and will not repent, Thou art a priest for ever, after the order of Melchisedek."

CEREMONIES AND CHARGES UPON THE INSTALLATION OF THE OFFICERS OF A ROYAL ARCH CHAPTER.

1. *The Grand Officers will meet at a convenient place, and open.*

2. *The subordinate Chapter will meet in the outer courts of their Hall, and form an avenue for the reception of the Grand Officers.*

3. *When formed, they will dispatch a committee to the place where the Grand Officers are assembled, to inform the Grand Marshal that the Chapter is prepared to receive them;—the Grand Marshal will announce the committee, and introduce them to the Grand Officers.*

4. *The Grand Officers will move in procession, conducted by the committee, to the Hall of the Chapter, in the following order:*

Grand Tyler;
Two Grand Stewards;
Representatives of subordinate Chapters, according to seniority, by threes triangular;
Three Great Lights;
Orator, Chaplain, and other Clergy;
Grand Secretary, Grand Treasurer, and Grand Royal Arch Captain;
Grand P. Sojourner, Grand Captain of the Host, and Deputy Grand High Priest;
Grand Scribe, Grand King, and Grand High Priest;
(Grand Marshal, on the left of the Procession.)

N. B. The Grand P. Sojourner, Grand Captain of the Host, and Grand Royal Arch Captain, are appointed pro tempore.

When the Grand High Priest enters, the grand honors are given.

5. *The Grand Secretary will then call over the names of the officers elect; and the Grand High Priest will ask whether they accept their respective offices. If they answer in the affirmative, he then asks the members whether they remain satisfied with their choice.* If they answer in the affirmative, he directs their officers to

approach the sacred volume, and become qualified for Installation, agreeably to the 4th section of the 4th article of the General Grand Royal Arch Constitution.

6. The Grand Marshal will then form the whole in procession, and they will march through the *veils* into the inner apartment, where they will surround the altar, which is previously prepared in *ample form* for the occasion.

7. All present will kneel, and the following prayer will be recited.

Prayer.

Almighty and Supreme High Priest of heaven and Earth! Who is there in heaven but thee! and who upon earth can stand in competition with thee! Thy OMNISCIENT Mind brings all things in review, past, present and to come; thine OMNIPOTENT Arm directs the movements of the vast creation; thine OMNIPRESENT Eye pervades the secret recesses of every heart; thy boundless beneficence supplies us with every comfort and enjoyment; and thine unspeakable perfections and glory surpass the understanding of the children of men! Our Father, who art in heaven, we invoke thy benediction upon the purposes of our present assembly. Let this Chapter be established to thine honor: let its officers be endowed with wisdom to discern, and fidelity to pursue, its true interests; let its members be ever mindful of the duty they owe to their God, the obedience they owe to their superiors, the love they owe to their equals, and the good will they owe to all mankind. Let this Chapter be consecrated to thy glory, and its members ever exemplify their love to God by their beneficence to man.

"Glory be to God on high."

Response. "Amen! So mote it be."

They are then qualified in due form.

All the Companions, except High Priests and Past High Priests, are then desired to withdraw, while the new High Priest is solemnly bound to the performance of his duties; and after the performance of other necessary ceremonies, not proper to be written, they are permitted to return.

8. *The whole then repair to their appropriate stations; when the Grand Marshal will form a general procession, in the following order:*

Captain of the Host;

Three Royal Arch Stewards, with Rods;
Tyler of a Blue Lodge;
Entered Apprentices;
Fellow Crafts;
Master Masons;
Stewards of Lodges, having Jewels;
Deacons having Jewels;
Secretaries having Jewels;
Treasurers having Jewels;
Wardens having Jewels;
Mark Master Masons;
M. E. Masters;
Royal Arch Masons by three;
Royal Masters by three;
Select Masters by three;
Orders of Knighthood;
Tyler of the new Chapter;

Members of the new Chapter, by three;
Three Masters of Veils;
Secretary, Treasurer, R. A. Captain, and
P. Sojourner carrying the Ark;
A Companion carrying the Pot of Incense;
Two Companions carrying Lights;
Scribe, High Priest and King;
Grand Chapter, as before prescribed.

On arriving at the church or house where the services are to be performed, they halt, open to the right and left, and face inward, while the Grand Officers and others in succession pass through and enter the house.

9. *The officers and members of the new Chapter, and also of the Grand Chapter, being seated, the Grand Marshal proclaims silence, and the ceremonies commence.*

10. *An Anthem or Ode is to be performed.*

11. *An Oration or Address is to be delivered.*

12. *An Ode or Piece of Music.*

*[13. *The Deputy Grand High Priest then rises and informs the Grand High Priest, that "a number of Companions, duly instructed in the sublime mysteries, being desirous of promoting the honor, and propagating the principles of the Art, have applied to the Grand Chapter for a warrant to constitute a new Chapter of Royal Arch Masons, which having been obtained, they are now assembled for the purpose of being constituted, and having their officers installed in due and ancient form.*]

---

* NOTE. Those paragraphs which are enclosed within brackets, apply exclusively to cases when new Chapters are constituted, and their officers installed for the first time. The rest apply equally to such cases, as well as to annual Installations.

[14. *The Grand Marshal will then form the officers and members of the new Chapter in front of the Grand Officers; after which, the Grand High Priest directs the Grand Secretary to read the warrant.*]

[15. *The Grand High Priest then rises and says, "By virtue of the high powers in me vested, I do form you, my respected Companions, into a regular Chapter of Royal Arch Masons. From henceforth you are authorized and empowered to open and hold a Lodge of Mark Masters, Past Masters, and Most Excellent Masters, and a Chapter of Royal Arch Masons; and to do and perform all such things as thereunto may appertain; conforming, in all your doings, to the General Grand Royal Arch Constitution, and the general regulations of the State Grand Chapter. And may the God of your fathers be with you, guide and direct you in all your doings."*]

16. *The furniture, clothing, jewels, implements, utensils, &c. belonging to the Chapter, (having been previously placed in the centre, in front of the Grand Officers, covered,) are now uncovered, and the new Chapter is dedicated in due and ancient form.*

17. *The Dedication then follows: the Grand Chaplain saying,*

"To our Most Excellent Patron ZERUBBABEL, we solemnly dedicate this Chapter. May the blessing of our Heavenly High Priest descend and rest upon its members, and may their felicity be immortal.

"Glory be to God on high."

[Response by the Companions.]

"As it was in the beginning, is now, and ever shall be, world without end! Amen.

"So mote it be."

18. *The Grand Marshal then says, "I am directed to proclaim, and I do hereby proclaim this Chapter, by the name of ——— Chapter, duly consecrated, constituted and dedicated. This," &c. &c.*

19. *An Ode.*

20. *The Deputy Grand High Priest will then present the first officer of the new Chapter to the Grand High Priest, saying,*

MOST EXCELLENT GRAND HIGH PRIEST,

I present you my worthy Companion —— ———, nominated in the warrant, to be installed High Priest of this [new] Chapter. I find him to be skilful in the royal art, and attentive to the moral precepts of our forefathers, and have therefore no doubt but he will discharge the duties of his office with fidelity.

The Grand High Priest then addresses him as follows:

MOST EXCELLENT,

I feel much satisfaction in performing my duty on the present occasion, by installing you into the office of High Priest of this [new] Chapter. It is an office highly honorable to all those who diligently perform the important duties annexed to it. Your reputed Masonic knowledge, however, precludes the necessity of a particular enumeration of those duties. I shall therefore only observe, that by a frequent recurrence to the constitution, and general regulations, and constant practice of the several sublime lectures and charges, you will be best able to fulfill them; and I am confident that the

Companions who are chosen to preside with you, will give strength to your endeavors, and support to your exertions.——I shall now propose certain questions to you, relative to the duties of your office, and to which I must request your unequivocal answer.

1. Do you solemnly promise that you will redouble your endeavors to correct the vices, purify the morals, and promote the happiness of those of your Companions, who have attained this sublime degree?

2. That you will never suffer your Chapter to be opened, unless there be present nine regular Royal Arch Masons?

3. That you will never suffer either more or less than three brethren to be exalted in your Chapter at one and the same time?

4. That you will not exalt any one to this degree, who has not shown a charitable and humane disposition; or who has not made a considerable proficiency in the foregoing degrees?

5. That you will promote the general good of our order, and, on all proper occasions, be ready to give and receive instructions, and particularly from the General and State Grand Officers?

6. That, to the utmost of your power, you will preserve the solemnities of our ceremonies, and behave, in open Chapter, with the most profound respect and reverence, as an example to your Companions?

7. That you will not acknowledge or have intercourse with any Chapter that does not work under a constitutional warrant or dispensation?

8. That you will not admit any visitor into your Chapter, who has not been exalted in a Chapter legally constituted, without his being first formally healed?

9. That you will observe and support such byelaws as may be made by your Chapter, in conformity to the General Grand Royal Arch Constitution, and the general regulations of the Grand Chapter?

10. That you will pay respect and due obedience to the instructions of the General and State Grand Officers, particularly relating to the several Lectures and Charges, and will resign the chair to them, severally, when they may visit your Chapter?

11. That you will support and observe the General Grand Royal Arch Constitution, and the General Regulations of the Grand Royal Arch Chapter, under whose authority you act?

Do you submit to all these things, and do you promise to observe and practice them faithfully?

These questions being answered in the affirmative the Companions all kneel in due form, and the Grand High Priest or Grand Chaplain repeats the following, or some other suitable prayer.

"Most holy and glorious Lord God, the Great High Priest of Heaven and Earth,

"We approach thee with reverence, and implore thy blessing on the Companion appointed to preside over this new assembly, and now prostrate before thee;—, fill his heart with thy fear, that his tongue and actions may pronounce thy glory. Make him steadfast in thy service; grant him firmness of mind; animate his heart, and strengthen his endeavors; may he teach thy judgments and thy laws; and may the incense he shall put before thee, upon thine altar, prove an acceptable sacrifice unto thee. Bless him, O Lord, and bless the work of his hands.—Accept us in mercy; hear thou from Heaven thy dwelling-place, and forgive our transgressions.

"Glory be to God the Father; as it was in the beginning," &c.

[Response.] "So mote it be."

21. *The Grand High Priest will then cause the High Priest elect to be invested with his clothing, badges, &c.; after which he will address him as follows, viz.*

MOST EXCELLENT,

In consequence of your cheerful acquiescence with the charges, which you have heard recited, you are qualified for installation as the High Priest of this Royal Arch Chapter; and it is incumbent upon me, on this occasion, to point out some of the particulars appertaining to your office, duty and dignity.

All legally constituted bodies of Royal Arch Masons, are called Chapters; as regular bodies of masons of the preceding degrees, are called Lodges. Every Chapter ought to assemble for work, at least once in three months; and must consist of a High Priest, King, Scribe, Captain of the Host, Principal Sojourner, Royal Arch Captain, three Grand Masters of the Veils, Treasurer, Secretary, and as many members as may be found convenient for working to advantage.

The officers of the chapter officiate in the lodges, holden for conferring the preparatory degrees, according to rank, as follows: viz.

The High Priest, as Master.

The King, as Senior Warden.

The Scribe, as Junior Warden.

The Captain of the Host, as Marshal or Master of Ceremonies.

The Principal Sojourner, as Senior Deacon,

The Royal Arch Captain, as Junior Deacon.

The Master of the first Veil, as Junior Overseer.

The Master of the second Veil, as Senior Overseer.

The Master of the third Veil, as Master Overseer.

The Treasurer, Secretary, Chaplain, Stewards, and Tyler, as officers of corresponding rank.

The High Priest of every Chapter has it in special charge, to see that the bye-laws of his Chapter, as well as the General Grand Royal Arch Constitution, and all the regulations of the Grand Chapter, are duly observed:—that all the officers of his Chapter perform the duties of their respective offices faithfully, and are examples of diligence and industry to their companions;—that true and accurate records of all the proceedings of the chapter are kept by the secretary;—that the treasurer keeps and renders exact and just accounts of all the monies and other property belonging to the Chapter;—that the regular returns be made annually to the Grand Chapter;—and that the annual dues to the Grand Chapter be regularly and punctually paid. He has the right and authority of calling his Chapter together at pleasure, upon any emergency or occurrence, which in his judgment may require their meeting. It is his privilege and duty, together with the king and scribe, to attend the meetings of the Grand Chapter, either in person or by proxy; and the well-being of the institution requires that his duty should on no occasion be omitted.

The office of High Priest is a station highly honorable to all those, who diligently perform the important duties annexed to it. By a frequent recurrence to the constitution and general regulations, and a constant practice of the several sublime lectures and charges, you will be best enabled to fulfill those duties; and I am confident that the companions, who are chosen to preside with you, will give strength to your endeavors, and support to your exertions.

Let the *Mitre* with which you are invested, remind you of the dignity of the office you sustain, and its inscription impress upon your mind a sense of your dependence upon God;—that perfection is not given unto man upon earth, and that perfect holiness belongeth alone unto the Lord.

The *Breast-Plate,* with which you are decorated, in imitation of that upon which were engraven the names of the twelve tribes, and worn by the High Priest of Israel, is to teach you that you are always to bear in mind your responsibility to the laws and ordinances of the institution, and that the honor and interests of your Chapter and its members, should be always near your heart.

The *various colors* of the *Robes* you wear are emblematical of every grace and virtue which can adorn and beautify the human mind; each of which will be briefly illustrated in the course of the charges to be delivered to your subordinate officers.

You will now take charge of your officers, standing upon their right, and present them severally in succession to the Deputy Grand High Priest, by whom they will be presented to me for installation.

22. *The High Priest of the Chapter will then present his second officer to the Deputy Grand High Priest, who will present him to the Grand High Priest in the words of the Constitution. The Grand High Priest,*

will then ask him whether he has attended to the ancient charges and regulations before recited to his superior officer: if he answers in the affirmative, he is asked whether he fully and freely assents to the same: if he answers in the affirmative, the Grand High Priest directs his deputy to invest him with his clothing, &c. and then addresses him as follows, viz.

CHARGE to the Second Officer, or King.

EXCELLENT COMPANION,

The important station to which you are elected in this Chapter, requires from you exemplary conduct; its duties demand your most assiduous attention; you are to second and support your chief in all the requirements of his office; and should casualties at any time prevent his attendance, you are to succeed him in the performance of his duties.

Your badge (the Level surmounted by a crown) should remind you, that although you are the representative of a King, and exalted by office above your Companions, yet that you remain upon a level with them, as respects your duty to God, to your neighbor, and to yourself; that you are equally bound with them, to be obedient to the laws and ordinances of the institution, to be charitable, humane and just, and to seek every occasion of doing good.

Your office teaches a striking lesson of humility. The institutions of political society teach us to consider the king as the chief of created beings, and that the first duty of his subjects, is to obey his mandates:—but the institutions of our sublime degrees, by placing the King in a situation subordinate to the High Priest, teaches us that our duty to God is paramount to all other duties, and should ever claim the priority of our obedience to man; and that however strongly we may be bound to obey the laws of civil society, yet that those laws, to be just, should never intermeddle with matters of conscience, nor dictate articles of faith.

The *Scarlet Robe,* an emblem of imperial dignity, should remind you of the paternal concern you should ever feel for the welfare of your Chapter, and the *fervency* and *zeal* with which you should Endeavour to promote its prosperity.

In presenting to you the Crown, which is an emblem of royalty, I would remind you, that to reign sovereign in the hearts and affections of men, must be far more grateful to a generous and benevolent mind, than to rule over their lives and fortunes; and that to enable you to enjoy this preeminence with honor and satisfaction, you must subject your own passions and prejudices to the dominion of reason and charity.

You are entitled to the second seat in the council of your Companions. Let the bright example of your illustrious predecessor in the Grand Council at Jerusalem, stimulate you to the faithful discharge of your duties; and when the King of kings shall summon you into his immediate presence, from his hand may you receive a *crown of glory,* which shall never fade away.

23. *The King will then retire to the line of officers, and the Scribe will be presented in the manner before mentioned. After his investiture, the Grand High Priest will address him as follows, viz.*

CHARGE to the Third Officer, or Scribe.

EXCELLENT COMPANION,

The office of Scribe, to which you are elected, is very important and respectable. In the absence of your superior officers, you are bound to succeed them, and to perform their duties. The purposes of the institution ought never to suffer for want of intelligence in its proper officers; you will therefore perceive the necessity there is of your possessing such qualifications as will enable you to accomplish those duties which are incumbent upon you, in your appropriate station, as well as those which may occasionally devolve on you, by the absence of your superiors.

The *Purple Robe,* with which you are invested, is an emblem of *union,* and is calculated to remind you that the harmony and unanimity of the Chapter should be your constant aim; and to this end you are studiously to avoid all occasions of giving offence, or countenancing any thing that may create divisions or dissentions. You are, by all means in your power, to Endeavour to establish a permanent union and good understanding among all orders and degrees of masonry; and, as the glorious sun, at its meridian height, dispels the mist and clouds which obscure the horizon, so may your exertions tend to dissipate the gloom of jealousy and discord, whenever they may appear.

Your badge (*a Plumb-rule surmounted by the Turban,*) is an emblem of rectitude and vigilance; and while you stand as a watchman upon the tower, to guard your Companions against the approach of those enemies of human felicity, *intemperance* and *excess,* let this faithful monitor ever remind you to walk uprightly in your station; admonishing and animating your Companions to fidelity and industry while at labour, and to temperance and moderation while at refreshment.—And, when the Great Watchman of Israel, whose eye never slumbers nor sleeps, shall relieve you from your post on earth, may he permit you in heaven to participate in that food and refreshment which is

"Such as the saints in glory love,
"And such as angels eat."

24. *The Scribe will then retire to the line of officers, and the next officer be presented as before.*

CHARGE to the Fourth Officer, or Captain of the Host.

COMPANION,

The office with which you are entrusted, is of high importance, and demands your most zealous consideration. The preservation of the most essential traits of our ancient customs, usages and landmarks, are within your province; and it is indispensably necessary, that the part assigned to you, in the immediate practice of our rites and ceremonies, should be perfectly understood, and correctly administered.

Your office corresponds with that of marshal, or master of ceremonies. You are to superintend all processions of your Chapter, when moving as a distinct body, either in public or private; and as the world can only judge of our private discipline by our public deportment, you will be careful that the utmost order and decorum be observed on all such occasions. You will ever be attentive to the commands of your chief, and always near at hand to see them duly executed. I invest you with the badge of your office, and presume that you will give to your duties all that study and attention which their importance demands.

25. *He will then retire to the line of officers, and the next officer will be presented.*

CHARGE to the Fifth Officer, or Principal Sojourner.

COMPANION,

The office confided to you, though subordinate in degree, is equal in importance to any in the Chapter, that of your chief alone excepted. Your office corresponds with that of *senior deacon,* in the preparatory degrees. Among the duties required of you, the preparation and introduction of candidates are not the least. As in our intercourse with the world, experience teaches that first impressions are often the most durable, and the most difficult to eradicate; so it is of great importance, in all cases, that those impressions should be correct and just: hence it is essential that the officer, who brings the blind by a way that they knew not, and leads them in paths that they have not known, should always be well qualified to make darkness light before them, and crooked things strait.

Your *Robe of Office* is an emblem of humility; and teaches that in the prosecution of a laudable undertaking, we should never decline taking any part that may be assigned us, although it may be the most difficult or dangerous.

The *rose-coloured tesselated Border,* adorning the robe, is an emblem of ardour and perseverance, and signifies, that when we have engaged in a virtuous course, notwithstanding all the impediments, hardships, and trials, we may be destined to encounter, we should endure them all with fortitude, and ardently persevere unto the end; resting assured of receiving, at the termination of our labors, a noble and glorious reward. Your past exertions will be considered as a pledge of your future assiduity in the faithful discharge of your duties.

26. *He will then retire to the line of officers, and the next officer is presented.*

CHARGE to the Sixth Officer, or Royal Arch Captain.

COMPANION,

The well-known duties of your station require but little elucidation. Your office in the preparatory degrees corresponds with that of *junior deacon.* It is your province, conjointly with the Captain of the Host, to attend the examination of all visitors, and to take care that none are permitted to enter the Chapter, but such as have *traveled the rugged path* of trial, and evinced their title to our favor and friendship. You will be attentive to obey the commands of the Captain of the Host, during *the introduction of strangers among* the workmen; and should they be permitted to pass your post, may they by him be introduced into the presence of the Grand Council.

The *White Banner,* entrusted to your care, is emblematical of that purity of heart and rectitude of conduct, which ought to actuate all those who pass the white veil of the sanctuary. I give it to you strongly in charge, never to suffer any one to pass your post, without the *signet of truth.*

I present you the badge of your office, in expectation of your performing your duties with intelligence, assiduity and propriety.

27. *He then retires, and the Three Grand Masters of the Veils are presented together.*

CHARGE to the Master of the Third Veil.

COMPANION,

I present you with the *Scarlet Banner,* which is the ensign of your office, and with a sword to protect and defend the same. The rich and beautiful color of your banner is emblematical of *fervency* and *zeal;* it is the appropriate color of the Royal Arch degree; it admonishes us, that we should be fervent in the exercise of our devotions to God, and zealous in our endeavors to promote the happiness of man.

CHARGE to the Master of the Second Veil.

COMPANION,

I invest you with the *Purple Banner,* which is the ensign of your office, and arm you with a sword, to enable you to maintain its honor.

The color of your banner is produced by a due mixture of *blue* and *scarlet;* the former of which is the characteristic color of the *symbolic* or *first three degrees of masonry,* and the latter, that of the *royal arch degree.* It is an emblem of *union,* and is the characteristic color of the intermediate degrees. It admonishes us to cultivate and improve that spirit of union and harmony, between the brethren of the symbolic degrees and the companions of the sublime degrees, which should ever distinguish the members of a society founded upon the principles of everlasting truth and universal philanthropy.

CHARGE to the Master of the First Veil.

COMPANION,

I invest you with the *Blue Banner,* which is the ensign of your office, and a sword for its defense and protection. The color of your banner is one of the most durable and beautiful in nature. It is the appropriate color adopted and worn by our ancient brethren of the three symbolic degrees, and is the *peculiar characteristic* of an institution which has stood the test of ages, and which is as much distinguished by the durability of its materials or principles, as by the beauty of its superstructure. It is an emblem of universal *friendship* and benevolence; and instructs us, that in the mind of a mason those virtues should be as expansive as the blue arch of heaven itself.

CHARGE to the three Masters of the Veils, as Overseers.

COMPANIONS,

Those who are placed as overseers of any work should be well qualified to judge of its beauties and deformities, its excellencies and defects; they should be capable of estimating the former, and amending the latter. This consideration should induce you to cultivate and improve all those qualifications with which you are already endowed, as well as to persevere in your endeavors to acquire those in which you are deficient. Let the various *colors* of the *banners* committed to your charge, admonish you to the exercise of the several virtues of which they are emblematic; and you are to enjoin the practice of those virtues upon all who shall present themselves, or the *work* of their hands, *for* your *inspection.* Let no work receive your approbation, but such as is calculated to adorn and strengthen the Masonic edifice. Be industrious and faithful in practicing and disseminating knowledge of the *true and perfect work,* which alone can stand the test of the *Grand Overseer's Square,* in the great day of trial and retribution. Then, although every *rod* should become a *serpent,* and every serpent an enemy to this institution, yet shall their utmost exertions to destroy its reputation, or sap its foundation, become as impotent as the *leprous hand,* or as *water spilled upon the ground,* which cannot be gathered up again.

28. *They then retire, and the Treasurer is presented.*

CHARGE to the Treasurer.

COMPANION,

You are elected Treasurer of this Chapter, and I have the pleasure of investing you with the badge of your office. The qualities which should recommend a Treasurer, are *accuracy* and *fidelity;* accuracy, in keeping a fair and minute account of all receipts and disbursements; fidelity, in carefully preserving all the property and funds of the Chapter, that may be placed in his hands, and rendering a just account of the same, whenever he is called upon for that purpose. I presume that your respect for the institution, your attachment to the interests of your Chapter, and your regard for a good name, which is better than precious ointment, will prompt you to the faithful discharge of the duties of your office.

29. *He then retires, and the Secretary is presented.*

CHARGE to the Secretary.

COMPANION,

I with pleasure invest you with your badge as Secretary of this Chapter. The qualities which should recommend a Secretary, are, *promptitude* in issuing the notifications and orders of his superior officers; *punctuality* in attending the convocations of the Chapter; *correctness* in recording their proceedings; *judgment* in discriminating between what is proper and what is improper to be committed to writing; *regularity* in making his annual returns to the Grand Chapter; *integrity* in accounting for all monies that may pass through his hands; and *fidelity* in paying the same over into the hands of the treasurer. The possession of these good qualities, I presume, has designated you a suitable candidate for this important office; and I cannot entertain a doubt that you will discharge its duties beneficially to the Chapter, and honorably to yourself. And when you shall have completed the record of your transactions here below, and finished the term of your probation, may you be admitted into the celestial Grand Chapter of saints and angels, and find your name *recorded* in the *book of life eternal.*

30. *He then retires, and the Chaplain is presented.*

CHARGE to the Chaplain.

"E. AND REV. COMPANION,

"You are appointed Chaplain of this Chapter; and I now invest you with this circular jewel, the badge of your office. It is emblematical of eternity, and reminds us that here is not our abiding place. Your inclination will undoubtedly conspire with your duty, when you perform in the Chapter those solemn services which created beings should constantly render to their infinite CREATOR;

and which, when offered by one whose holy profession is, "to point to heaven and lead the way," may, by refining our morals, strengthening our virtues, and purifying our minds, prepare us for admission into the society of those above, whose happiness will be as endless as it is perfect."

31. *He then retires, and the Stewards are presented.*

CHARGE to the Stewards.

COMPANIONS,

You being elected Stewards of this Chapter, I with pleasure invest you with the badges of your office. It is your province to see that every necessary preparation is made for the convenience and accommodation of the Chapter, previous to the time appointed for meeting. You are to see that the clothing, implements and furniture of each degree respectively, are properly disposed, and in suitable array for use, whenever they may be required, and that they are secured, and proper care taken of them, when the business of the Chapter is over. You are to see that necessary refreshments are provided, and that all your companions, and particularly visitors, are suitably accommodated and supplied. You are to be frugal and prudent in your disbursements and to be careful that no extravagance or waste is committed in your department; and when you have faithfully fulfilled your stewardship here below, may you receive from heaven the happy greeting of "Well done, good and faithful servants."

32. *They then retire, and the Tyler is presented.*

CHARGE to the Tyler.

COMPANION,

You are appointed Tyler of this Chapter, and I invest you with the badge, and this implement of your office. As the sword is placed in the hands of the Tyler, to enable him effectually to guard against the approach of all *cowans and eavesdroppers,* and suffer none to pass or repass but such as are *duly qualified;* so it should morally serve as a constant admonition to us to set a guard at the entrance of our thoughts; to place a watch at the door of our lips; to post a sentinel at the avenue of our actions; thereby excluding every unqualified and unworthy thought, word and deed; and preserving consciences void of offence towards God and towards man.

As the first application from visitors for admission into the Chapter is generally made to the Tyler at the door, your station will often present you to the observation of strangers: it is therefore essentially necessary that he who sustains the office with which you are entrusted, should be a man of good morals, steady habits, strict discipline, temperate, affable, and discreet. I trust that a just regard for the honor and reputation of the institution will ever induce you to perform with fidelity the trust reposed in you; and when the door of this earthly tabernacle shall be closed, may you find an abundant entrance through the gates into the temple and city of our God.

33. *He will then retire, and then follows an*

ADDRESS to the High Priest.

M. E. COMPANION,

Having been honored with the free suffrages of the members of this Chapter, you are elected to the most important office which is within their power to bestow. This expression of their esteem and respect should draw from you corresponding sensations; and your demeanor should be such as to repay the honor they have so conspicuously conferred upon you, by an honorable and faithful discharge of the duties of your office. The station you are called to fill, is important, not only as it respects the correct practice of our rites and ceremonies, and the internal economy of the Chapter over which you preside; but the public reputation of the institution will be generally found to rise or fall according to the skill,

Fidelity, and discretion, with which its concerns are managed, and in proportion as the characters and conduct of its principal officers are estimable or censurable You have accepted a trust, to which is attached a weight of responsibility that will require all your efforts to discharge honorably to yourself, and satisfactorily to the Chapter. You are to see that your officers are capable and faithful in the exercise of their offices. Should they lack ability, you are expected to supply their defects; you are to watch carefully the progress of their performances, and to see that the long established customs of the institution suffer no derangement in their hands. You are to have a careful eye over the general conduct of the Chapter; see that due order and subordination is observed on all occasions; that the members are properly instructed; that due solemnity be observed in the practice of our rites; that no improper levity be permitted at any time, but more especially at the *introduction of strangers among the workmen.*

In fine, you are to be an example to your officers and members, which they need not hesitate to follow; thus securing to yourself the favor of Heaven, and the applause of your brethren and companions.

ADDRESS to the Officers generally.

COMPANIONS IN OFFICE,

Precept and example should ever advance with equal pace. Those moral duties which you are required to teach unto others, you should never neglect to practice yourselves.

Do you desire that the demeanor of your equals and inferiors towards you should be marked with deference and respect? Be sure that you omit no opportunity of furnishing them with examples in your own conduct towards your superiors. Do you desire to obtain instruction from those who are wiser or better informed than yourselves? Be sure that you are always ready to impart of your knowledge to those within your sphere, who stand in need of, and are entitled to receive it. Do you desire distinction among your companions? Be sure that your claims to preferment are founded upon superior attainments; let no ambitious passion be suffered to induce you to envy or supplant a companion who may be considered as better qualified for promotion than yourselves; but rather let a laudable emulation induce you to strive to excel each other in improvement and discipline; ever remembering, that he, who faithfully performs his duty, even in a subordinate or private station, is as justly entitled to esteem and respect, as he who is invested with supreme authority.

ADDRESS to the Chapter at large.

COMPANIONS,

The exercise and management of the sublime degrees of masonry in your Chapter hitherto, are so highly appreciated, and the good reputation of the Chapter so well established, that I must presume these considerations alone were there no others of greater magnitude, would be sufficient to induce you to preserve and perpetuate this valuable and honorable character. But when to these is added the pleasure which every philanthropic heart must feel in doing good, in promoting good order, in diffusing light and knowledge, in cultivating Masonic and Christian charity, which are the great objects of this sublime institution, I cannot doubt that your future conduct, and that of your successors, will be calculated still to increase the luster of your justly esteemed reputation.

May your *chapter* become *beautiful* as the *temple, peaceful* as the *ark,* and *sacred* as its *most holy place.* May your oblations of *piety* and *praise* be *grateful* as the *incense;* your love *warm* as its *flame,* and your charity diffusive as its fragrance. May your hearts be *pure* as the *altar,* and your conduct *acceptable* as the *offering.* May the exercises of your *charity* be as constant as the returning wants of the distressed *widow* and helpless *orphan.* May the approbation of Heaven be your encouragement and the testimony of a good conscience your support: may you be endowed with every good and perfect gift, while *traveling* the *rugged path* of life, and finally be *admitted within the veil* of heaven, to the full enjoyment of life eternal. So mote it be. Amen.

34. *The officers and members of the Chapter will then pass in review in front of the Grand Officers, with their hands crossed on their breasts, bowing as they pass.*

35. *The Grand Marshal will then proclaim the Chapter, by the name of ————, to be regularly constituted, and its officers duly installed.*

36. *The ceremonies conclude with an Ode, or appropriate piece of music.*

37. *The procession is then formed, when they return to the place from whence they set out.*

38. *When the Grand Officers retire, the Chapter will form an avenue for them to pass through, and salute them with the grand honors. The two bodies then separately close their respective Chapters.*

CONSTITUTION

OF THE

General Grand Royal Arch Chapter

OF THE

UNITED STATES OF AMERICA.

ARTICLE I.

OF THE GENERAL GRAND CHAPTER.

SECT. 1. **THERE** shall be a General Grand Chapter of Royal Arch Masons for the United States of America, which shall be holden as is hereinafter directed, and shall consist of a General Grand High Priest, Deputy General Grand High Priest, General Grand King, General Grand Scribe, Secretary, Treasurer, Chaplain, and Marshal; and likewise of the several Grand and Deputy Grand High Priests, Kings, and Scribes, for the time being, of the several State Grand Chapters, under the jurisdiction of this General Grand Chapter; and of the Past General Grand High Priests, Deputy General Grand High Priests, Kings, and Scribes, of the said General Grand Chapter; and the aforesaid officers, or their proxies, shall be the only members and voters in said General Grand Chapter. And no person shall be constituted a proxy, unless he be a present or past officer of this or a State Grand Chapter.

SECT. 2. The General Grand Chapter shall meet septennially, on the second Thursday in September, for the choice of officers, and other business: dating from the second Thursday in September, A. D. 1805, at such place as may, from time to time, be appointed.

SECT. 3. A special meeting of the General Grand Chapter shall be called whenever the General Grand High Priest, Deputy General Grand High Priest, General Grand King, and General Grand Scribe, or any two of them, may deem it necessary; and also whenever it may be required by a majority of the Grand Chapters of the States aforesaid, provided such requisition be made known in writing, by the said Grand Chapters respectively, to the General Grand High Priest, Deputy General Grand High Priest, King or Scribe.—And it shall be the duty of the said General Officers, and they are each of them severally authorized, empowered and directed, upon receiving official notice of such requisition from a majority of the General Grand Chapters aforesaid, to appoint a time and place of meeting, and notify each of the State Grand Chapters thereof accordingly.

SECT. 4. It shall be incumbent on the General Grand High Priest, Deputy General Grand High Priest, General Grand King, and General Grand Scribe, severally, to improve and perfect themselves in the sublime Arts, and work of Mark Masters, Past Masters, Most Excellent Masters, and Royal Arch Masons; to make themselves Masters of the several Masonic Lectures and Ancient Charges;—to consult with each other, and with the Grand and Deputy Grand High Priests, Kings and Scribes of the several States aforesaid, for the purpose of adopting measures suitable and proper for diffusing a knowledge of the said Lectures and Charges, and an uniform mode of *working,* in the several Chapters and Lodges throughout this jurisdiction; and the better to effect this laudable purpose, the aforesaid General Grand Officers are severally hereby authorized, and empowered, to visit and preside in any and every Chapter of Royal Arch Masons, and Lodge of Most Excellent, Past, or Mark Master Masons, throughout the said States, and to give such instructions and directions as the good of the Fraternity may require; always adhering to the ancient landmarks of the order.

SECT. 5. In all cases of the absence of any Officer from any body of masons, instituted or holden by virtue of this Constitution, the Officer next in rank shall succeed his superior; unless through courtesy said Officer should decline in favor of a past superior Officer present.—And in case of the absence of all the Officers from any legal meeting of either of the bodies aforesaid, the Members present, according to seniority and abilities, shall fill the several Offices.

SECT. 6. In every Chapter or Lodge of Masons, instituted or holden by virtue of this Constitution, all questions (except upon the admission of members or candidates) shall be determined by a majority of votes; the presiding Officer for the time being, being entitled to vote, if a Member; and in case the votes should at any time be equally divided, the presiding Officer as aforesaid, shall give the casting vote.

SECT. 7. The General Grand Royal Arch Chapter shall be competent (on concurrence of two thirds of its members present) at any time hereafter, to revise, amend and alter this Constitution.

SECT. 8. In case any casualty should, at any time hereafter, prevent the septennial election of Officers, the several General Grand Officers shall sustain their respective Offices until successors are duly elected and qualified.

SECT. 9. The General Grand High Priest, Deputy General Grand High Priest, General Grand King, and General Grand Scribe, shall severally have power and authority to institute new Royal Arch Chapters, and Lodges of the subordinate degrees, in any State in which there is not a Grand Chapter regularly established. But no new Chapter shall be instituted in any State wherein there is a Chapter or Chapters holden under the authority of this Constitution, without a recommendation from the Chapter nearest the residence of the petitioners.—The fees for instituting a new Royal Arch Chapter, with the subordinate degrees, shall be ninety dollars; and for a new Mark Master's Lodge, twenty dollars; exclusive of such compensation to the Grand Secretary, as the Grand Officers aforesaid may deem reasonable.

ARTICLE II.

OF THE STATE GRAND ROYAL ARCH CHAPTERS.

SECT. 1. The STATE GRAND CHAPTERS shall severally consist of a Grand High Priest, Deputy Grand High Priest, Grand King, Grand Scribe, Grand Secretary, Grand Treasurer, Grand Chaplain, and Grand Marshal, and likewise of the High Priests, Kings and Scribes, for the time being, of the several Chapters over which they shall respectively preside, and of the Past Grand and Deputy Grand High Priests, Kings and Scribes of the said Grand Chapters; and the said enumerated Officers (or their proxies) shall be the only members and voters in the said Grand Chapters respectively.

SECT. 2. The State Grand Chapters shall severally be holden at least once in every year, at such times and places as they shall respectively direct; and the Grand or Deputy Grand High Priests respectively, for the time being, may at any time call a special meeting, to be holden at such place as they shall severally think proper to appoint.

SECT. 3. The Officers of the State Grand Chapters shall be chosen annually, by ballot, at such time and place as the said Grand Chapters shall respectively direct.

SECT. 4. The several State Grand Chapters (subject to the provisions of this Constitution) shall have the sole government and superintendence of the several Royal Arch Chapters, and Lodges of Most Excellent, Past and Mark Master Masons, within their respective jurisdictions; to assign their limits, and settle controversies that may happen between them;—and shall have power, under their respective seals, and the sign manual of their respective Grand or Deputy Grand High Priests, Kings and Scribes, (or their legal proxies,) attested by their respective Secretaries, to constitute new Chapters of Royal Arch Masons, and Lodges of Most Excellent, Past, and Mark Master Masons, within their respective jurisdictions.

SECT. 5. The Grand and Deputy Grand High Priests severally, shall have the power and authority, whenever they shall deem it inexpedient, (during the recess of the Grand Chapter of which they are officers,) to grant Letters of Dispensation, under their respective hands, and private seals, to a competent number of petitioners (possessing the qualifications required by the 9th Section of the 2d Article,) empowering them to open a Chapter of Royal Arch Masons, and Lodge of Most Excellent, Past and Mark Master Masons, for a certain specified term of time: provided, that the said term of time shall not extend beyond the next meeting of the Grand Chapter of the State in which such Dispensation shall be granted; and provided further, that the same fees as are required by this Constitution for Warrants, shall be first deposited in the hands of the Grand Treasurer.—And in all cases of such Dispensations, the Grand or Deputy Grand High Priests respectively, who may grant the same, shall make report thereof, at the next stated meeting of the Grand Chapter of their respective jurisdictions, when the said Grand Chapters, respectively, may either continue or recall the said Dispensations, or may grant the petitioners a warrant of Constitution: And in case such warrant shall be granted, the fees first deposited, shall be credited in payment for the same; but if a warrant should not be granted, nor the dispensation continued, the said fees shall be refunded to the petitioners, excepting only such part thereof as shall have been actually expended by means of their application.

SECT. 6. The several State Grand Chapters shall possess authority, upon the institution of new Royal Arch Chapters, or Lodges of Mark Masters, within their respective jurisdictions, to require the payment of such fees as they may deem expedient and proper; which said fees shall be advanced and paid into the Treasury before a warrant or charter shall be issued.

SECT. 7. No warrant shall be granted, for instituting Lodges of Most Excellent or Past Masters, independent of a Chapter of Royal Arch Masons.

SECT. 8. The Grand Chapters severally, shall have power to require from the several Chapters and Lodges under their respective jurisdictions, such reasonable proportion of sums, received by them for the exaltation or advancement of candidates, and such certain annual sums from their respective members, as by their ordinances or regulations shall hereafter be appointed; all which said sums or dues shall be made good, and paid annually, by the said Chapters and Lodges respectively, into the Grand Treasury of the Grand Chapter under which they hold their authority, on or before the first day of the respective annual meetings of the said Grand Chapters.

SECT. 9. No warrant for the institution of a new Chapter of Royal Arch Masons shall be granted, except upon the petition of nine regular Royal Arch Masons; which petition shall be accompanied by a certificate from the Chapter nearest to the place where the new Chapter is intended to be opened, vouching for the moral characters, and Masonic abilities, of the petitioners, and recommending to the Grand Chapter under whose authority they act, to grant their prayer. And no warrant for the institution of a Lodge of Mark Master Masons shall be granted, except upon the petition of (at least) five regular Mark Master Masons, accompanied by vouchers from the nearest Lodge of that degree, similar to those required upon the institution of a Chapter.

SECT. 10. The Grand Secretaries of the State Grand Chapters shall severally make an annual communication to each other, and also to the General Grand Secretary, containing a list of Grand Officers and all such other matters as may be deemed necessary for the mutual information of the said Grand Chapters. And the said Grand Secretaries shall also regularly transmit to the General Grand Secretary, a copy of all their bylaws and regulations.

SECT. 11. Whenever there shall have been three, or more, Royal Arch Chapters, instituted in any State, be virtue of authority derived from this Constitution, a Grand Chapter may be formed in such State, (with the approbation of one or more of the General Grand Officers,) by the High Priests, Kings and Scribes of the said Chapters, who shall be authorized to elect the Grand Officers. Provided always, that no new State Grand Chapter shall be formed until after the expiration of one year from the establishment of the junior Chapter in such State.

SECT. 12. The several Grand and Deputy Grand High Priests, Kings and Scribes, for the time being, of the several State Grand Chapters, are bound to the performance of the same duties, and are invested with the same powers and prerogatives, throughout their respective jurisdictions, as are prescribed to the General Grand Officers, in the 4th Section, 1st Article, of this Constitution.

SECT. 13. The jurisdiction of the several State Grand Chapters shall not extend beyond the limits of the State in which they shall respectively be holden.

ARTICLE III.

OF THE SUBORDINATE CHAPTERS AND LODGES.

SECT. 1. All legally constituted assemblies of Royal Arch Masons are called CHAPTERS; as regular bodies of Mark Masters, Past Masters, and Most Excellent Masters, are called LODGES. Every Chapter ought to assemble for work at least once in every three months; and must consist of an High Priest, King, Scribe, Captain of the Host, Principal Sojourner, Royal Arch Captain, three Grand Masters, Secretary, Treasurer, and as many Members as may be found convenient for working to advantage.

SECT. 2. Every Chapter of Royal Arch Masons, and Lodge of Mark Master Masons, throughout this jurisdiction, shall have a Warrant of Constitution from the Grand Chapter of the State in which they may respectively be holden, or a Warrant from one of the General Grand Officers. And no Chapter or Lodge shall be deemed legal without such warrant; and Masonic communication (either public or private) is hereby interdicted and forbidden, between any Chapter or Lodge under this jurisdiction, or any member of either of them, and any Chapter, Lodge or Assembly, that may be so illegally formed, opened or holden, without such warrant, or any or either of their members, or any person exalted or advanced in such illegal Chapter or Lodge. But nothing in this Section shall be construed to affect any Chapter or Lodge which was established before the adoption of the Grand Royal Arch Constitution at Hartford, (on the 27th day of January, A. D. 1798.)

SECT. 3. Whenever a Warrant is issued for instituting a Chapter of Royal Arch Masons, with a power in said Warrant to open and hold a Lodge of Most Excellent, Past, and Mark Master Masons, the High Priest, King and Scribe, for the time being, of such Chapter, shall be the Master and Wardens in said Lodges, according to seniority.

SECT. 4. All applications for the exaltation or advancement of Candidates, in any Chapter or Lodge, under this jurisdiction, shall lie over, at least one meeting, for the consideration of the members.

SECT. 5. No mason shall be a member of two separate and distinct bodies, of the same denomination, at one and the same time.

SECT. 6. No Chapter shall be removed, without the knowledge of the High Priest, nor any motion made for that purpose in his absence; but if the High Priest be present, and a motion is made and seconded, for removing the Chapter to some more convenient place, (within the limits prescribed in their Warrant,) the High Priest shall forthwith cause notifications to be issued to all the members, informing them of the motion for removal, and of the time and place when the question is to be determined; which notice shall be issued at least ten days previous to the appointed meeting. But if the High Priest (after motion duly made and seconded as aforesaid) should refuse or neglect to cause the notices to be issued as aforesaid, the officer next in rank, who may be present at the next regular meeting following, (upon motion made and seconded for that purpose,) may in like manner issue the said notices.

SECT. 7. All Mark Master Masons' Lodges shall be regulated, in cases of removal, by the same rules as are prescribed in the foregoing Section for the removal of Chapters.

SECT. 8. The High Priest, and other Officers, of every Chapter, and the Officers of every Lodge of Mark Master Masons, shall be chosen annually, by ballot.

SECT. 9. The High Priest of every Chapter has it in special charge, as appertaining to his office, duty and dignity, to see that the by-laws of his Chapter, as well as the General Grand Royal Arch Constitution, and the General Regulations of the Grand Chapter, be duly observed; that all the other Officers of his Chapter perform the duties of their respective offices faithfully, and are examples of diligence and industry to their companions;—that true and exact records be kept of all the proceedings of the Chapter by the Secretary; that the Treasurer keep and render exact and just accounts of all the monies belonging to the Chapter; that regular returns be made by the Secretary, annually, to the Grand Chapter, of all admissions of candidates or members; and that the annual dues to the Grand Chapter be regularly and punctually paid.—He has the special care and charge of the Warrant of his Chapter.—He has the right and authority of calling his Chapter at pleasure, upon any emergency or occurrence which in his judgment may require their meeting; and he is to fill the chair when present. It is likewise his duty, together with his King and Scribe, to attend the meetings of the Grand Chapter (when duly summoned by the Grand Secretary) either in person, or by proxy.

SECT. 10. For the preservation of secrecy and good harmony, and in order that due decorum may be observed while the Chapter is engaged in business, a worthy Royal Arch Mason is to be appointed from time to time for tyling the Chapter. His duty is fixed by custom, and known in all regular Chapters.—He may be elected annually, but is to continue in office only during good behavior, and is to be paid for his services.

SECT. 11. All Lodges of Mark Master Masons are bound to observe the two preceding articles, as far as they can be applied to the government of a *Lodge*.

SECT. 12. No Chapter shall confer the degrees of Mark Master Mason, Past Master, Most Excellent Master, and Royal Arch Mason, upon any Brother, for a less sum than Twenty Dollars.—And no Lodge of Mark Master Masons shall advance a Brother to that degree, for a less sum than Four Dollars.

SECT. 13. When either of the Officers or Members of the General Grand Chapter, or any of the State Grand Chapters, cannot personally attend their respective meetings, they shall severally have the authority to constitute a proxy, which proxy shall have the same right to a seat and vote as his constituent.

ARTICLE IV.

OF CONSTITUTING NEW CHAPTERS.

SECT. 1. [See Order of High Priesthood, from page 125 to 156.]

SECT. 2. At the institution of all Lodges of Mark Master Masons, under this jurisdiction, the same ceremonies as are prescribed in the foregoing section are to be observed, as far as they will apply to that degree.

SECT. 3. Whenever it shall be inconvenient for the General Grand Officers, or the Grand or Deputy Grand High Priests, respectively, to attend in person, to constitute a new Chapter or Lodge, and install the Officers, they shall severally have power and authority to appoint some worthy High Priest, or Past High Priest, to perform the necessary ceremonies.

SECT. 4. The Officers of every Chapter and Lodge under this jurisdiction, before they enter upon the exercise of their respective Offices, and also the members of all such Chapters and Lodges, and every candidate upon his admission into the same, shall take the following obligation, viz. "I, A. B. do promise and swear that I will support and maintain the General Grand Royal Arch Constitution."

1 HEREBY certify that the foregoing is a true copy of the General Grand Royal Arch Constitution for the United States of America, as altered, amended and ratified, at a meeting of the General Grand Chapter, begun and holden at New-York, in the State of New-York, on the 6th day of June, A. D. 1816.

Witness,

JOHN ABBOT, *G. G. Secretary.*

OFFICERS

OF THE

General Grand Royal Arch Chapter

OF THE

UNITED STATES OF AMERICA,

As elected at their last Septennial Assembly, in the City of New-York, and State of New-York, on Friday, September 10*th, A. D.* 1819, *and of Royal Arch Masonry* 2349.

M. E. and Hon. DEWITT CLINTON, of Albany, New-York, General Grand High Priest.

M. E. HENRY FOWLE, Esq. of Boston, Massachusetts, Deputy General Grand High Priest.

M. E. JOHN SNOW, Esq. of Worthington, Ohio, General Grand King.

M. E. PHILIP P. ECKEL, Esq. of Baltimore, Maryland, General Grand Scribe.

M. E. PETER GRINNEL, Esq. of Providence, Rhode-Island, General Grand Treasurer.

M. E. JOHN ABBOT, Esq. of Westford, Massachusetts, General Grand Secretary.

M. E. and Rev. JONATHAN NYE, of Newfane, Vermont, General Grand Chaplain.

M. E. DAVID G. COWAN, Esq. of Danville, Kentucky, General Grand Marshal.

A LIST OF GRAND CHAPTERS,

Under the jurisdiction of the General Grand Royal Arch Chapter of the United States of America.

ALSO,

A List of Subordinate Chapters,

Holding their Charter or Warrant from under the same authority.

MAINE.

The Grand Chapter of Maine, and all subordinate Chapters. Their Grand Convocation is held at Portland, annually.

NEW-HAMPSHIRE.

The Grand Chapter of New-Hampshire, and all subordinate Chapters. Their Grand Convocation is held at Concord, on the second Wednesday of July, annually.

MASSACHUSETTS.

The Grand Chapter of Massachusetts, and all subordinate Chapters. Their Grand Convocations are held alternately at Boston and Newburyport, on the first Tuesday of February, and second Tuesday of September, annually.

RHODE-ISLAND.

The Grand Chapter of Rhode-Island, and all subordinate Chapters. Their Grand Convocation is held at Providence, annually.

CONNECTICUT.

The Grand Chapter of Connecticut, and all subordinate Chapters. Their Grand Convocation is held annually, on the second Thursday following the first Wednesday of May, at Hartford and New-Haven alternately, beginning at New-Haven, 1820.

VERMONT.

The Grand Chapter of Vermont, and all subordinate Chapters. Their Grand Convocations are held at Rutland, on the third Wednesday of June, annually.

NEW-YORK.

The Grand Chapter of New-York, and all subordinate Chapters. Their Grand Convocation is held at Albany, on the first Tuesday of February, annually.

NEW-JERSEY.

Washington Chapter, No. 1, Newark. New-Brunswick Chapter, No. 2, New-Brunswick. Brearly Chapter, No. 3, Bridgetown, under the Grand Chapter of Pennsylvania.

MARYLAND and D. C.

The Grand Chapter of Maryland and District of Columbia, and all subordinate Chapters. Their Grand Convocation is held at Baltimore, annually.

NORTH-CAROLINA.

The Grand Chapter of North-Carolina, and all subordinate Chapters. Their Grand Convocations are held alternately at Fayetteville and Tarborough, on the first Monday of December, annually.

SOUTH-CAROLINA.

The Grand Chapter of South-Carolina, and all subordinate Chapters. Their Grand Convocations are held at Charleston, on the last Wednesday of February annually.

GEORGIA.

The Grand Chapter of Georgia, and all subordinate Chapters. Their Grand Convocations are held at Louisville, on the first Monday of May, annually.

KENTUCKY.

The Grand Chapter of Kentucky, and all subordinate Chapters. Their Grand Convocations are held at Frankfort, on the first Monday of December, annually.

OHIO.

The Grand Chapter of Ohio, and all subordinate Chapters. The Grand Convocations are held at Columbus, on Wednesday, succeeding the second Monday of December, annually.

MICHIGAN TERRITORY.

Monroe Chapter, No. 1, Detroit.

TENNESSEE.

Cumberland Chapter, No. 1, Nashville.

MISSISSIPPI.

Natchez Chapter, No. 1, Natchez.

INDIANA.

Madison Chapter, No. 1, Madison.

Brockville Chapter, No. 2, Brockville.

MISSOURI.

Missouri Chapter, No. 1, St. Louis.

ALABAMA.

——— Chapter, No. 1, Tuscaloosa.

MASONIC SONGS.

ENTERED APPRENTICES' SONG.

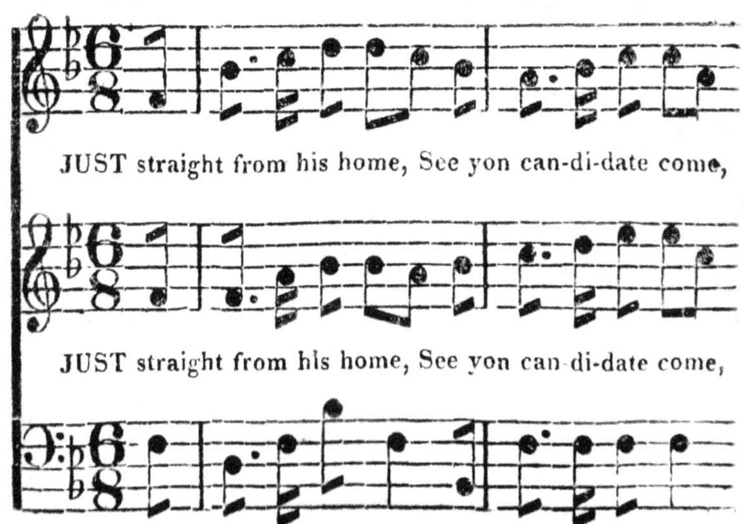

Pre-par'd for the time and oc - ca - sion:
Pre-par'd for the time and oc - ca - sion:
Of all that can harm, We will him dis - arm,
Of all that can harm, We will him dis arm,
That he no way may hurt a Free Ma - son.
That he no way may hurt a Free Ma - son.

His eyes cannot search
Out the way of his march,
Nor yet where his steps he must place on:
When him we receive,
He cannot perceive
How he came to be made a Free Mason.

Then he'll danger defy,
And on Heaven rely
For strength to support the occasion,
With the blessing of pray'r
He banishes fear,
And undaunted is made a Free Mason.

When he makes his demand,
By the master's command,
To know if he's fit for the station,
Around he is brought,
Ere he get what he sought
From a free and an accepted Mason.

When girded with care,
By the help of the square,
The emblem of truth and of reason,
In form he is plac'd,
While to him are rehears'd
The mysteries of a Free Mason;

Then full in his sight
Doth shine the grand light,
To illumine the works which we trace on;
And now, as his due,
He's cloth'd in full view
With the badge of an accepted Mason.

Now hark! we enlarge
On the duties and charge,
Where his conduct and walk he must place on.
Then our rites we'll fulfill,
And show our good will
To a free and an accepted Mason.

FELLOW CRAFT'S SONG.

CHORUS.
Hail! mys-te-rious, Hail, glo-rious Ma-son-ry!
Hail! mys-te-rious, Hail, glo-rious Ma-son-ry!
Hail! mys-te-rious, Hail, glo-rious Ma-son-ry!

tr
That makes us ev - - - - er great and free.
tr
That makes us ev - - - - er great and free.
That makes us ev - - - - er great and free.

In vain mankind for shelter sought,
In vain from place to place did roam,
Until from Heaven, from Heaven he was taught
To plan, to build, to fix his home.

Illustrious hence we date our Art,
And now in beauteous piles appear,
We shall to endless, to endless time impart,
How worthy and how great we are.

Nor we less fam'd for every tie,
By which the human thought is bound;
Love, truth, and *friendship,* and friendship socially,
Join all our hearts and hands around.

Our actions still by Virtue blest,
And to our precepts ever true,
The world admiring, admiring shall request
To learn, and our bright paths pursue.

MASTER'S SONG.

BY A BROTHER.

Beneath the blue and starry zone,
Whose arch high swelling girds the pole,
The Master on his *orient throne*
Unfolds to view the mystic roll;
At once the pure fraternal soul
Bends to the *sign* with sacred awe,
And reads upon the letter'd scroll
In words of light, the unutter'd *law.*

Let us our hearts and hands entwine
And form one perfect wreath of *love;*
Then kneeling at the voice divine
That spake to mortals from above,
Put on the meekness of the dove
And the white robes of *charity,*
And in unerring wisdom prove
Our brethren with the single eye.

Be there no darkling scowl of hate
Upon the calm unruffled brow,
But each in innocence elate
To Virtue's brightness only bow:
Blest guardian of all pleasures! Thou
Be ever at our Master's side,
And mark with radiant finger how
Thy *words* can be our only guide.

By thee conducted we ascend
The *steps* that lead alone to Heaven
And where the mounting arches end
To each the *sign* of *worth* is given;
Then mantled by the shades of even
We meet beneath the unclouded sky,
And bind the links no power hath riven,
In which we swear to live and die.

Let us these favored hours employ,
These moments of the social night
To sing the silver song of joy,
And make the chain of *union* bright;
So may we even here unite
To spend the hours in mercy given,
Led by the *tokens* which invite
Alone to happiness and Heaven.

MASTER'S SONG.

BY BROTHER T. S. WEBB.

Not those who at our meet-ings
Hear lec - tures 'gainst their will,
DUET.
MEZZA VOCE.
But on - ly those whose plea - sure,
At ev'-ry lodge can be, T'im-prove them-selves by
lec - tures, In glo-rious Ma - son - ry.

The faithful, worthy brother,
    Whose heart can feel for grief,
Whose bosom with compassion
    Steps forth to its relief,

Whose soul is ever ready,
Around him to diffuse
The principles of Masons,
And guard them from abuse;
Chorus. These are thy sons, whose pleasure,
At every lodge, will be,
T'improve themselves by lectures
In glorious Masonry.
Hail! glorious Masonry.

King Solomon, our patron,
Transmitted this command—
"The faithful and praise-worthy
True light must understand;
And my descendants, also,
Who 're seated in the *East,*
Have not fulfill'd their duty,
Till light has reach'd the *West.*"
Chorus. Therefore, our highest pleasure,
At every lodge, should be,
T'improve ourselves by lectures
In glorious Masonry.
Hail! glorious Masonry.

The duty and the station,
Of master in the chair,
Obliges him to summon
Each brother to prepare;
That all may be enabled,
By slow, though sure degrees,
To answer in rotation,
With honor and with ease.
Chorus. Such are thy sons, whose pleasure,
At every lodge, will be,
T'improve themselves by lectures
In glorious Masonry.
Hail! glorious Masonry.

THE MASON'S ADIEU.

WORDS BY BURNS.

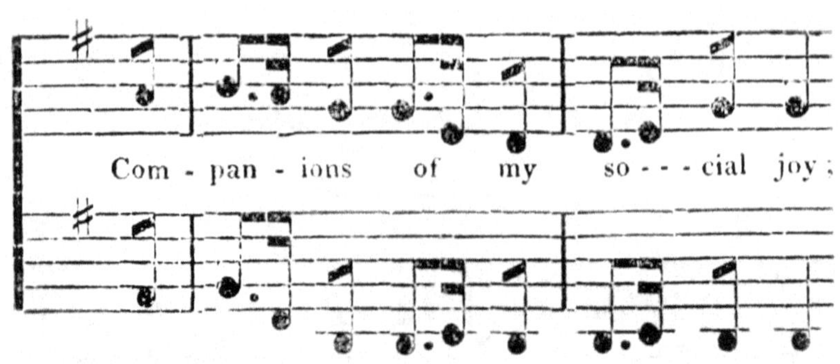
Com - pan - ions of my so - - - cial joy ;

Though I to for - - eign lands must hie,

Pur - - - su - - ing for - - tune's slipp' - ry ba';

With melt - ing heart and brim - - ful eye,

Oft have I met your social band,
To spend a cheerful, festive night,
Oft, honour'd with supreme command,
Presiding o'er the sons of light:
And by that hieroglyphic bright,
Which none but craftsmen ever saw,
Strong mem'ry on my heart shall write,
Those happy scenes when far awa'.

May freedom, harmony, and love,
Cement you in the grand design,
Beneath th' Omniscient Eye above,
The glorious Architect divine:
That you may keep th' unerring line,
Still guided by the plummet's law,
'Till order bright completely shine,
Shall be my pray'r when far awa'.

And you, farewell, whose merits claim
Justly that highest badge to wear,
May Heaven bless your noble name,
To Masonry and friendship dear:
My last request permit me then,
When yearly you're assembled a',
One round, I ask it with a tear,
To him, your friend, that's far awa'.

And you, kind-hearted sisters, fair,
I sing farewell to all your charms,
Th' impression of your pleasing air
With rapture oft my bosom warms.
Alas! the social winter's night
No more returns while breath I draw,
Till sisters, brothers, all unite,
In that Grand Lodge that's far awa'.

ODE FOR GRAND VISITATION.

WORDS BY R. T. PAINE, ESQ.

tell the Art, which guides the spheres, Bless'd Ma - son-
tell the Art, which guides the spheres, Bless'd Ma - son-
tell the Art, which guides the spheres, Bless'd Ma - son-

PIA.
ry, all hail! With na-ture's birth thy laws be - gan
ry, all hail!
ry, all hail! With na-ture's birth thy laws be - gan

To rule on earth fra - ter - nal man, And still in
To rule on earth fra - ter - nal man, And still in

FOR.
heav'n pre-vail. With na-ture's birth thy laws be - gan
With na-ture's birth thy laws be - gan
heav'n pre-vail. With na-ture's birth thy laws be-gan

To rule on earth fra - ter - nal man, And
To rule on earth fra - ter - nal man,
To rule on earth fra - ter - nal man, And

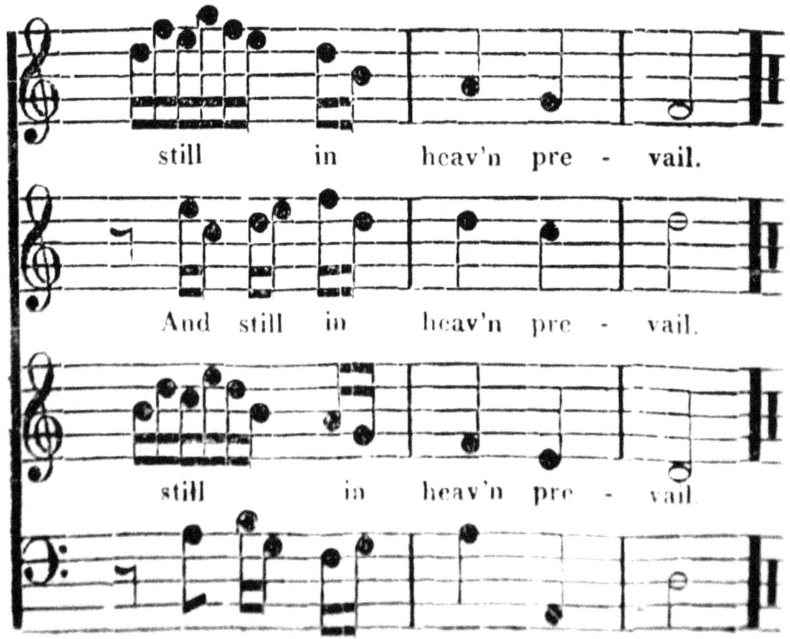
still in heav'n pre - vail.
And still in heav'n pre - vail.
still in heav'n pre - vail.

O'er matter's modes thy mystic sway
Can fashion Chaos' devious way,
    To order's lucid maze;
Can rear the cloud-assaulting tow'r,
And bid the worm, that breathes its hour,
    Its humble palace raise.

From nascent life to being's pride,
The surest boon thy laws provide,
    When wayward fate beguiles;
The tears thou shedst for human wo,
In falling shine like Iris' bow,
    And beam an arch of smiles.

Come, Priest of Science, truth array'd,
And with thee bring each tuneful maid,
    Thou lov'st on Shinar's plains;
Revive Creation's primal plan,
Subdue this wilderness of man,
    Bid social *virtue* reign.

HYMN FOR CONSECRATION.

Be - fore thy throne we bend, To
Be - fore thy throne we bend, To

us thy grace ex - tend, And to our
us thy grace ex - tend, And to our

O, hear our prayer to-day,
Turn not thy face away,
O Lord our God!
Heaven, thy dread dwelling place,
Cannot contain thy Grace,
Remember now our race,
O Lord our God!

God of our fathers, hear,
And to our cry be near,
Jehovah, God!
The Heavens eternal bow,
Forgive in mercy now
Thy suppliants here, O Thou,
Jehovah, God!

To Thee our hearts do draw,
On them O write thy law,
Our Savior, God!
When in this Lodge we're met,
And at thine Altar set,
O, do not us forget,
Our Savior, God!

ODE FOR DEDICATION.

BY J. H.

Kings! From thy ce - les - tial

courts a - - bove, Send beams of

grace on se - raph's wings; O,

may they, gilt with light di-

vine, Shed on our hearts in-

p p Expressive
tr
tr
spir - ing rays; While bend - ing

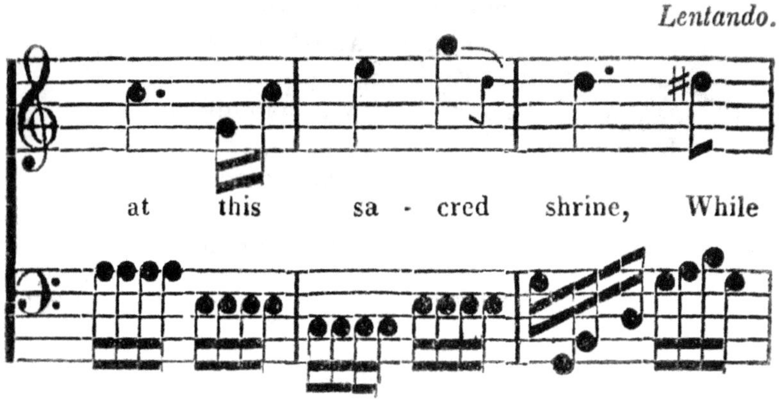
Lentando.
at this sa - cred shrine, While

Cres.
ad lib.
3
bend-ing at this sa - - - - cred shrine,

a tempo.
tr
We of-fer mys-tic songs of praise.

Faith! with divine and heav'nward eye;
    Pointing to radiant realms of bliss,
Shed here thy sweet benignity,
    And crown our works with happiness;
Hope! too, with bosom void of fear,
    Still on thy steadfast anchor lean,
O! shed thy balmy influence here,
    And fill our breasts with joy serene.

And thou, fair Charity! whose smile
    Can bid the heart forget its woe,
Whose hand can misery's care beguile,
    And kindness' sweetest boon bestow,
Here shed thy sweet soul-soothing ray;
    Soften our hearts, thou Power divine!
Bid the warm gem of pity play,
    With sparkling luster, on our shrine.

Thou, who art thron'd midst dazzling light,
    And wrapp'd in brilliant robes of gold,
Whose flowing locks of silv'ry white
    Thy age and honor both unfold,
Genius of Masonry! descend,
    And guide our steps by thy strict law;
O! swiftly to our temple bend,
    And fill our breasts with solemn awe.

GLEE.

ALLEGRO MA NON PRESTO.
PIA.
HAIL! mys te-rious, glo-rious sci-ence,

CRES.
Hail! mys - te - rious, glo - rious sci-ence,
Hail! mys - te - rious, glo - rious sci-ence,

FOR.
Hail! mys - te - rious, glo - rious sci - ence,
Hail! mys - te - rious, glo - rious sci - ence,
Which to dis - cord bids de - fi - ance,
Which to dis - cord bids de - fi - ance.
Har - mo - ny a - lone reigns here,
Har - mo - ny a - lone reigns here,

Har - mo - ny a - lone reigns here.
Har - mo - ny a - lone reigns here.
MEZZO FOR.
Come let's sing - - - - - -
Come let's sing to Him that
- - - - - - - - - -
rais'd us From the rug-ged path that maz'd us,

PIA.
To the light that we re - vere,
To the light that we re - vere,
FOR.
To the light that we re - vere.
To the light that we re - vere.
PIA.
Hail, mys - ter' - ous,
Hail, mys - ter' - ous, glor' - ous, sci - ence,

FOR.
Hail, mys-ter'-ous, Hail, mys-ter'-ous,
Hail, mys-ter'-ous, glor'-ous sci-ence, Hail, mys-ter'-ous,
glor'-ous sci-ence, Which to dis-cord gives de-
glor'-ous sci-ence, Which to dis-cord gives de-
PIA.
fi-ance, Har - mo - ny a - lone reigns here.
fi-ance, Har - mo - ny a - lone reigns here.

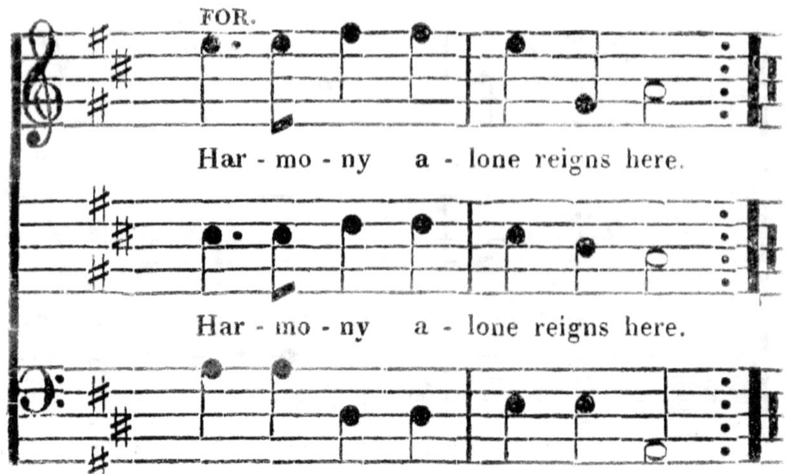

ODE TO CHARITY.

Music, see page 178.

OFFSPRING of Heav'n, mankind's best friend,
Bright Charity, inspire the lay;
On these celestial shores descend,
And quit the realms of cloudless day:
Chorus. To Thee our constant vows are paid,
Thy praise we hymn, Angelic Maid.

When Vulcan rages unconfin'd,
And Neptune mourns his baffled pow'r;
When flames aspiring with the wind,
To Heaven's high arch resistless tow'r:
Chorus. Tis thou our hearts with pity's glow,
Inspir'st to feel for human wo.

The house a dismal ruin lies,
Where mirth late tun'd her lyre of joy;
And tears of anguish fill your eyes,
Poor orphan girl, and houseless boy:—
Chorus. But thou, sweet maid, with pity's glow,
Inspir'st each heart to soothe their wo.

Come then, all-bounteous as thou art,
And hide thee from our sight no more;
Touch ev'ry soul, expand each heart,
That breathes on freedom's chosen shore
Chorus. Columbia's sons with pity's glow
Inspire to feel for human wo.

CHARITY.

A HYMN.

All ten - der, soft, and kind; A friend
All ten - der, soft, and kind; A friend
to all the hu - man race,
to all the hu - man race,
3
To all that's good and kind.
To all that's good and kind.

PIA.
The man of cha - ri - ty ex-
The man of cha - ri - ty ex-
tends To all his lib' - ral hand;
tends To all his lib' - ral hand;
FOR.
His kin-dred, neigh-bors, foes, and friends,
His kin-dred, neigh-bors, foes, and friends,

He aids the poor in their distress—
He hears when they complain;
With tender heart delights to bless
And lessen all their pain:
The sick, the prisoner, poor, and blind,
And all the sons of grief,
In him a benefactor find,
He loves to give relief.

'Tis love, that makes religion sweet,
'Tis love, that makes us rise,
With willing mind and ardent feet,
To yonder happy skies:
Then let us all in love abound,
And Charity pursue!
Thus shall we be with glory crown'd,
And love as angels do.

MASONIC HYMN.

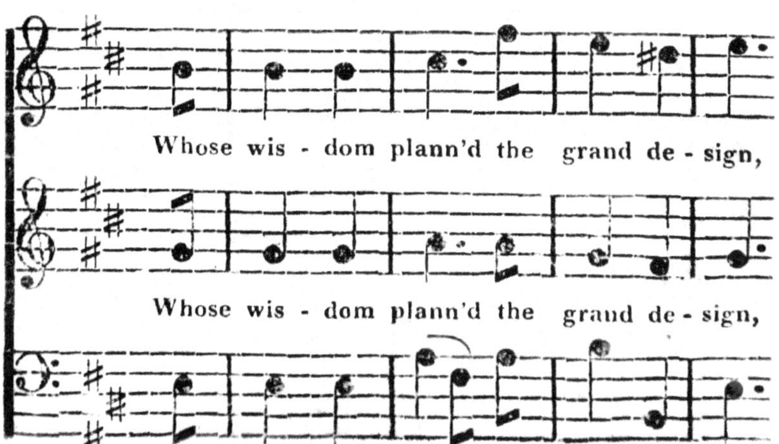

And gave to na - ture birth!
And gave to na - ture birth!
PIA.
Whose word with light a - dorn'd the skies,
Whose word with light a - dorn'd the skies,
CRES.
Gave mat - ter form, bade or - der rise,
Gave mat - ter form, bade or - der rise,

FOR.
And bless'd the new - born earth ;
And bless'd the new - born earth ;
CHORUS.
'Till love shall cease, 'till or - der dies,
'Till love shall cease, 'till or - der dies,
To Thee ma - son - ic praise shall rise.
To Thee ma - son - ic praise shall rise.
Repeat the last Chorus.

O, bless this love-cemented band,
Form'd and supported by thy hand,
For Charity's employ;
To shield the wretched from despair,
To spread through scenes of grief and care,
Reviving rays of joy.
Chorus. 'Till love, &c.

The lib'ral Arts, by Thee design'd,
To polish, comfort, aid mankind,
We labour to improve;
While we adore Jehovah's name,
Pour on our hearts the melting flame.
And mould our souls to love.
Chorus. Till love, &c.

FUNERAL HYMN.

MUSIC BY HANDEL.

ADAGIO.

tomb, Take this new treas-ure to
tomb, Take this new treas-ure to
thy trust And give these sa - cred
thy trust And give these sa - cred
re - lics room, To slum - ber
re - lics room, To slum - ber

In the si - lent dust.
In the si - lent dust.
And give these sa - cred
And give these sa - cred
rel - ics room To slum-ber
rel - ics room To slum-ber

Nor pain, nor grief, nor anxious fear,
Invade thy bounds; no mortal woes
Can reach the silent sleepers here,
And Angels watch their soft repose.

So Jesus slept; God's dying Son,
Past through the grave, and blest the bed;
Rest here, dear Saint, 'till from His throne
The morning break, and pierce the shade.

Break from his throne, illustrious Morn!
Attend, O Earth, his sov'reign Word!
Restore thy trust, a glorious form,
He must ascend to meet his Lord.

MOST EXCELLENT MASTER'S ODE.

MUSIC BY A. BROWN.

The heaven - ly Arch sub - lime - ly bent a - bove

And on the key stone blaz'd E - TER - NAL LOVE.

Heaven's favourite, man was made
In beauty fair,
Crime chang'd blest Eden's shade
To black despair;
Love from the sacred Arch came gently down,
Rais'd man from death, to an immortal crown.

Love, then, in chorus sing;
Hail Love divine!
Masons your *Cassia* bring
To deck his shrine;
Christians unite while Angels join in song,
All Earth and Heaven the glorious strain prolong.

ROYAL ARCH SONG.

BY A COMPANION.

MUSIC BY J. WHITAKER.

Joy! the secret *vault* is found;
Full the *sunbeam* falls within,
Pointing darkly under ground,
To the treasure we would win.
They have brought it forth to light,
And again it cheers the earth;
All its leaves are purely bright,
Shining in their newest worth.

This shall be the sacred *mark*
Which shall guide us to the skies,
Bearing, like a *holy ark,*
All the hearts who love to rise;
This shall be the *corner stone*
Which the builders threw away,
But was found the only one
Fitted for the *arch's* stay.

This shall be the *gavel* true,
At whose sound the crowd shall bend,
Giving to the *law* its due;
This shall be the faithful friend;
This the token, which shall bring
Kindness to the sick and poor,
Hastening on, on Angel's wing,
To the lone and *darksome door.*

This shall crown the mighty *arch,*
When the temple springs on high,
And the brethren bend their march
Wafting *incense* to the sky.
Then the solemn strain shall swell
From the bosom and the tongue,
And the Master's glory tell
In the harmony of song.

Here the exile, o'er the waste
Trudging homeward, shall repose;
All his toils and dangers past,
Here his long sojourning close
Entering through the sacred *veils*
To the holy cell he bends;
Then as sinking Nature fails,
Hope in glad fruition ends.

ROYAL ARCH SONG.

ANDANTE POMPOSO.

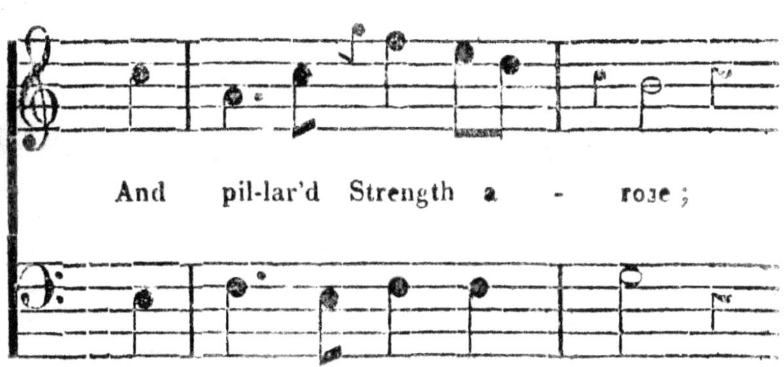

And Faith her man-sion chose ; Ex - ult - ing

bands the fa-bric view'd, Mys - ter' - ous

Pia. sf
pow'rs a - dor'd ; And high the Trip-ple

sf
Un-ion stood, And high the Trip - ple

Un - ion stood, That gave the mys - tic

word, - - - - - - That gave the mys-tic

word, - - - - - - - And high the Trip-ple

Un-ion stood, That gave the mys-tic word.

Pale Envy wither'd at the sight,
And, frowning o'er the pile,
Call'd *Murder* up from realms of night,
To blast the glorious toil.
With ruffian outrage join'd, in we
They form'd the league abhorr'd;
And wounded Science felt the blow,
That crush'd the *Mystic Word.*

Concealment, from sequester'd cave,
On sable pinions flew;—
And o'er the sacrilegious grave,
Her veil impervious threw,
The associate band, in solemn state,
The awful loss deplor'd;
And *Wisdom* mourn'd the ruthless fate,
That whelm'd the *Mystic Word.*

At length, through Time's expanded sphere
Fair Science speeds her way;
And warm'd by *Truth's* refulgence, clear
Reflects the kindred ray.
A second fabric's towering height,
Proclaims the *sign* restor'd;
From whose foundation, brought to light,
Is drawn the *Mystic Word.*

To depths obscure, the favour'd *Trine.*
A dreary course engage;
'Till, through the *Arch,* the ray divine
Illumes the *sacred page.*
From the wide wonders of this blaze,
Our ancient sign's restor'd;—
The *Royal Arch* alone displays
The long lost *Mystic Word.*

ROYAL ARCH SONG.

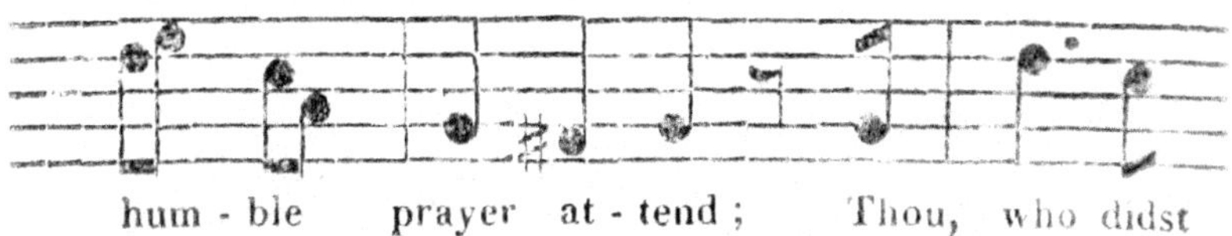

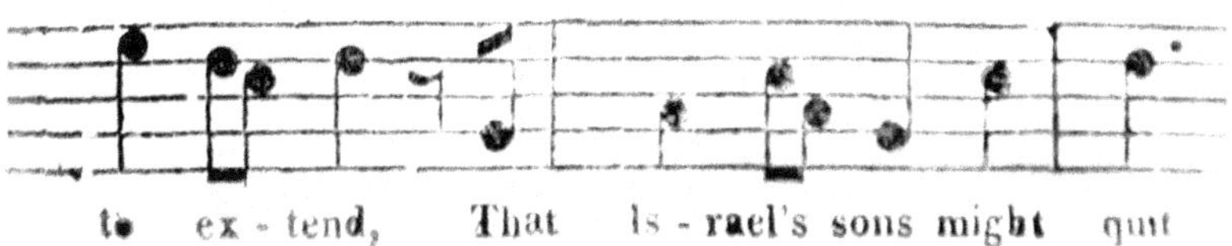

the land, Their ho - ly Tem - ple to at - tend ;

CHORUS. *For.*

All hail! great Ar-chi-tect di-vine! This u-ni-ver-sal
All hail! great Ar-chi-tect di-vine! This u-ni-ver-sal

frame is thine, This u-ni - ver-sal frame is thine,
frame is thine, This u-ni - ver-sal frame is thine,

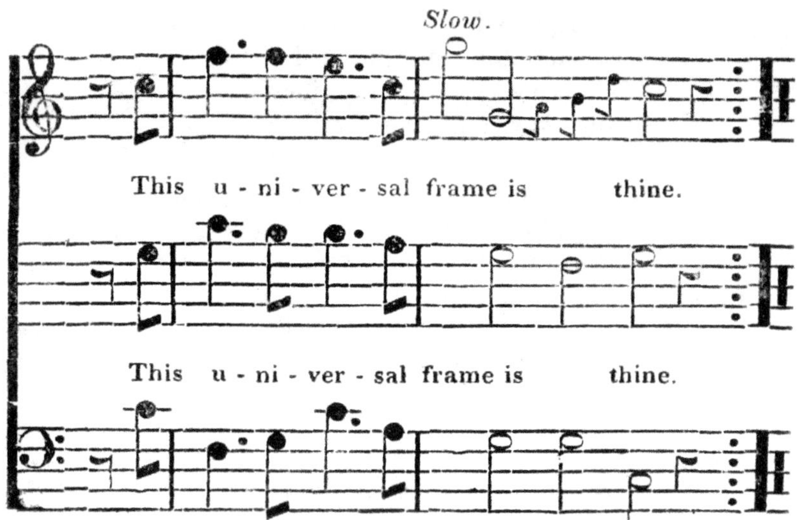

That sacred place, where Three in One
Compris'd thy comprehensive name,
And when the bright meridian Sun
Was seen thy glory to proclaim.
Thy watchful eye, a length of time,
The wond'rous circle did attend;
The glory and the power be thine,
Which shall from age to age descend.
Chorus. All hail, &c.

On thy Omnipotence we rest,
Secure of thy protection here;
And hope hereafter to be blest,
When we have left this world of care.
Grant us, great God, thy powerful aid
To Guide us through this vale of tears;
For where thy goodness is display'd,
Peace soothes the mind, and pleasure cheers.
Chorus. All hail, &c.

Inspire us with thy grace divine;
Thy sacred law our guide shall be;
To every good our hearts incline,
From every evil keep us free.
Our glad hosannas, Sovereign King!
Thy welcome here shall e'er proclaim,
And heaven's eternal arches ring
With thy revealed, holy Name:
Chorus. All hail! great Architect divine!
This universal frame is thine.

SELECT MASTER'S SONG.

BY A COMPANION.

HUNGARIAN AIR.

Now the work is completed and all are combin'd,
To close in the secret and deep-hidden cell
The words which are treasur'd as light to the mind,
Like the waters of truth in their close-cover'd well.
Here safely secured they shall live in the rock,
When the storm rages o'er it and levels the wall,
And still in the rage of the *conqueror's* shock,
The arches shall neither be shaken nor fall.

We have laid in its secret and silent retreat
The treasures that Kings shall exult to behold;
And the *pilgrim* shall hasten with ardour to meet
This gift, valued higher than jewels or gold:
Ages roll on their way and no foot shall be heard
In search of this roll to enlighten the world;
But a hand shall be found to recover the *Word,*
And then shall the standard of *truth* be unfurled.

We are seated in silence, and nothing can find
Its way to our distant and mystical cave;
And the *watchman* who guards not, our mandate shall bind
In the deeper concealment of *death* and the *grave*;
Be faithful and true, ever firm to your trust,
In the lesson we give in the council of light,
And the herald shall summon you forth from the dust,
Above in the meeting of souls to unite.

SELECT MASTER'S ANTHEM.

[*See Music, page* 213.]

"LET there be light," th' Almighty spoke;
Refulgent streams from chaos broke,
    To illume the rising earth!
Well pleas'd the Great JEHOVAH stood;
The Power Supreme pronounc'd it good,
    And gave the planets birth!

Chorus. In choral numbers masons join,
    To bless and praise this light divine.

Parent of light! accept our praise!
Who shedd'st on us thy brightest rays,
    The light that fills the mind:
By *choice selected,* lo! we stand,
By friendship join'd, a social band!
    That *love,* that *aid* mankind!

Chorus. In choral numbers, &c.

The *widow's* tear, the *orphan's* cry,
All wants our ready hands supply,
As far as power is given;
The naked clothe, the *pris'ner free,*
These are thy works, sweet *Charity!*
Reveal'd to us from Heaven.

Chorus. In choral numbers masons join,
To bless and praise this light divine.

SONG.

WRITTEN BY N. H. WRIGHT.

The bright eye of beauty may beam
With a light like the meteor glare;
But her victim may wake from his dream,
And hope may be chang'd to despair.

Like the rainbow, which shines from the cloud,
Her allurements awhile may deceive;
Till joy is enwrapp'd in a shroud,
And the mourner is left but to grieve.

But Friendship has charms, which endure,
Its birth was in regions above;
Tis a passion, like heaven, most pure,
For it sprang from the fountain of love.

Then let not the heart be depress'd
If one treat its fondness with scorn;
It may find in a Brother's warm breast
The rose that conceals not a thorn.

MASONIC ODE.

EMPIRES and kings have pass'd away,
Into oblivion's mine;
And tow'ring domes have felt decay,
Since auld lang syne.

But MASONRY, the glorious art,
With wisdom's ray divine;
'Twas ever so, the Hebrew cries,
In auld lang syne.

Behold the occidental chair
Proclaims the day's decline—
Hiram of Tyre was seated there,
In auld lang syne.

The *South* proclaims refreshment nigh
High twelve's the time to dine;
And *beauty* deck'd the southern sky,
In auld lang syne.

Yes, Masonry, whose temple here
Was built by hands divine,
Shall ever shine as bright and clear,
As auld lang syne.

Then brethren, for the worthy *three,*
Let us a wreath entwine,
The three great heads of Masonry
In auld lang syne.

Remembering oft that worthy one,
With gratitude divine,
The Tyrian youth—the widow's son
Of auld lang syne.

EPILOGUE.

AS lately, brethren, from the Lodge I came,
Warm'd with our royal order's purest flame;
Absorb'd in thought;—before my ravish'd eyes,
I saw the Genius, MASONRY, arise:
A curious hieroglyphic robe he wore,
And in his hand the sacred volume bore:
On one side was divine Astræa plac'd,
And soft-eyed Charity the other grac'd;
Humanity, the gen'ral friend was there,
And Pity, dropping the pathetic tear;
There too was Order;—there, with rosy mien,
Blithe Temp'rance shone, and white rob'd Truth was seen.
There, with a key suspended to his breast,
Silence appear'd; his lips his finger prest:
With these, soft warbling an instructive song,
Sweet Music, gaily smiling, tripp'd along.
Wild laughter, clam'rous noise, and mirth ill bred,
The brood of folly, at his presence fled.
The Genius spoke,—"My son, observe my train,
Which, of my order diff'rent parts explain.
Look up—behold the bright ASTRÆA there,
She will direct thee how to use the Square.
PITY will bid thee grieve, with those who grieve,
Whilst CHARITY will prompt thee to relieve;
Will prompt thee every comfort to bestow,
And draw the arrow from the breast of woe;
HUMANITY will lead to honour's goal,
Give the large thought, and form the gen'rous soul.
Will bid thee thy fraternal love expand,
To virtue of *all* faiths,—and ev'ry land.
ORDER will kindly teach her laws of peace,
Which discord stop, and social joys increase.

TEMP'RANCE instruct thee all excess t' avoid,
By which fair fame is lost, and health destroy'd:
TRUTH warn thee ne'er to use perfidious art,
And bid thy tongue be rooted in thy heart;
SILENCE direct thee never to disclose,
Whate'er thy brethren in thy breast repose;
For thee shall MUSIC strike the harmonious lyre,
And whilst she charms the ear, *morality* inspire.
These *all* observe;—and let thy conduct show,
What real blessings I on man bestow."
He said, and disappear'd;—and Oh! may we,
Who wear this honour'd badge, accepted, free,
To ev'ry grace and virtue temples raise,
And by our useful works our Order praise.

www.ingramcontent.com/pod-product-compliance
Lightning Source LLC
LaVergne TN
LVHW020537100826
845148LV00010B/1507
9781605320434